The Gates of Eternal Life

ADRIENNE VON SPEYR

The Gates of Eternal Life

TRANSLATED BY
SISTER CORONA SHARP

IGNATIUS PRESS   SAN FRANCISCO

Title of the German original:
Die Pforten des ewigen Lebens
© 1953 Johannes Verlag
Einsiedeln, Switzerland

Cover art (mosaic):
The Heavenly Jerusalem
S. Maria Maggiore, Rome, Italy
© Scala/Art Resource, New York

Cover design by Roxanne Mei Lum

With ecclesiastical approval
© 1983 Ignatius Press, San Francisco
All rights reserved
ISBN 978-0-89870-025-1
Library of Congress Number 82-84582
Printed in the United States of America ∞

Contents

1.	The Experience of Eternal Life	7
2.	The Gate of the Church's Year	23
3.	The Gate of Faith	35
4.	The Gate of the Sacraments	49
5.	The Gate of Ordination and the Consecrated Life	63
6.	The Gate of Prayer	77
7.	The Gate of Vision	89
8.	The Eternal Life of the Father and Creation	99
9.	The Eternal Life of the Son and Redemption	109
10.	The Eternal Life of the Spirit and Consummation	119
11.	The Presence of Eternal Life	127

1

The Experience of Eternal Life

"In the beginning God made heaven and earth." The first act by which we know the Father is the act of total change: it brings forth the world from chaos. The Father is revealed as the one who possesses the power and nature of creating, separating in order to create. In separating he creates, and in creating he sets in motion a process of alternation and differentiation. He separates solid from liquid, dark from light, heaven from earth. He shapes space, but also time. He introduces distinctions in created space, for the created world is not uniformity; rather, it can only be understood through the variety which God establishes in it from the outset, when he separates things from each other. Only by being isolated can things be distinguished—receiving with their existence individuality and a kind of alone-ness. Even day and night are mutually exclusive and mark the passing of time by their succession. It is a time that requires space in order to be grasped—when it is night here, it is day elsewhere—which forms a unity together with space, just as in space traces of time can be found.

The first human being created by God finds himself placed in this diversified world, which shows through its internal contrasts above all that it is not God. Adam knows God; knowledge of God is given to him through that which is not God, and which yet, in not being God, is a sign of his work and his presence. All that is not God has been created in a relationship to him; it exhibits the marks both of creatureliness and of its divine origin. Possibly time shows these elements most clearly, for it was created by someone outside time, who creates our time out of his own duration, which is not like our duration—who forms what is passing out of the eternal. He does not do so by introducing something imperishable into the perishable; rather, in creating what is perishable he makes possible the concept of the imperishable, which arises from the perishable as its contrary and complement.

It is not that God creates certain elements out of some eternal stuff, elements which, being finite and hence unworthy of the environs of eternity, fall from eternity to be subsumed under their own order. The temporal order is neither an overflow nor a waste product of eternity. The eternal God creates with his own divine powers, outside the eternal duration, a new, perishable duration. Outside the atmosphere of heaven he creates an atmosphere of earth and rivers and air. Outside the eternal light he creates a time of day and a time of night; and night does not derive from the eternal light, and day is not to be compared to the eternity of divine light. As Creator he creates it in an "outside", which is not inimical to eternity, only different from it, and good in itself. The Eternal One judges passing time and the differentiated oceans and lands, sky and earth, types of animals and human beings in their individuality: all of them he declares to be good. And man knows from this judgment of God that God is pleased with his work and sees it as right and perfect; and hence this creation offers man a means of existence appropriate to him because he too is found to be "good". Originally it was equally as appropriate to him as the eternal world of heaven is appropriate to the eternal Creator.

As soon as the first separation of day and night takes place, according to the creation story, God begins to count the days. A certain task is assigned to each day and completed on that same day. All things are conceived and arranged according to these days. A living relationship emerges between created things and time. In other words, from the beginning, God establishes all things in an order. Man too is created within this order, and is placed into it. Man is good, created and affirmed as such by God, and this quality imparts to him the world as his environment—this world which was created good and adapted to him. And since on the seventh day God rests, returns to his eternal heaven, withdraws from his work, man becomes conscious of being individual and alone, of being different and placed in a world that was planned for him and his use. He changes his course in favor of sin. When God again walks in Paradise, he can no longer judge man to be good. And man invents for himself a new relationship with God based on his being no longer good, a relationship corresponding to his new condition. God, however, punishes him by taking him out of his good environment and placing him in a world that matches his new condition. Now, for the first time, mutability becomes perishableness. Adam has moved away from the good and entered evil; therefore his life now is conditioned by what is perishable. Previously, he lived as a companion and partner of God; each time God approached him, there was a full encounter; God's coming did not surprise him, for at all times God found in him an appropriate expectation, a mirror image in which the original image could fulfill itself. In the new era there is no longer such a correspondence. The passage of time is now, in respect to man, a sign of a perishable existence. And man can no longer measure space and time according to the standard of original creation, but only according to that of his perishable state. All that was differentiated in the original order established by God now acquires another differentiation in a transitory order as a result of man's guilt. Formerly man, with his world, enjoyed a positive relationship with eternity, a self-confidence vis-à-vis this other world which nevertheless accompanied him through life. Now a gaping distance has intervened and man feels alien and excluded. He cannot measure or define this distance, but he experiences it as the sign of his lost goodness. And the more brightly the realization of the divine burns within him, the more clearly comes the feeling of being expelled. Man's relationship with God, which he had formerly accepted for what it was, God's unique gift, is now fraught with the knowledge of his own perishable and sinful state and of the remoteness, caused by guilt, which gives sharpness to the feeling of perishableness and makes it into a constant threat. Anyone who has experienced God in any way—man did so in the beginning, in such a way that the experience marked his inmost being—can no longer seek to understand his own being except in a relationship with God, and in God's intention and judgment.

Even in Paradise, in the perfect relationship

between man and God, there were particular times, particular meetings with God. At certain hours God walked in the garden; these hours belonged to God, and yet there was something within the time that God created which corresponded to them; man too in his own time-scheme could find a counterpart to them. Perhaps he could say: "On the first day of my life I met God, and on the fifth and seventh", without feeling separated from him or cast aside by him in the meantime. And no two meetings were the same, because some time intervened, and this time influenced and contributed God's next appearance, so that Adam, in his mutable life, through the succession of hours and days and what they contained, was involved in God's appearing. Consequently, all change was good; God accepted change since he chose to walk in time and make his appearance available to Adam as a temporal event. For Adam, this time did not offer any contradiction to God's eternity. As a creature, he did not experience the latter but only knew that it existed. He knew that God also existed outside of his walks in Paradise, the place where he was especially present for man. The life of God in Paradise was not opposed in any way to his life outside of Paradise. Certainly man experienced the meeting with God as a breakthrough into time, but it would never have occurred to him that for God it was also a pause, a change in his eternal time. Mutability was always on the side of man, whereas the unchangeable remained in God. God's walking was a flowing interaction between God and man, a distinction and yet no separation [*Unterscheidung*, distinction; *Scheidung*, separation]. Separation appears only when God expels the sinner from Paradise. In Paradise, Adam's time was open to receive God and his entire mystery; as a result, most of existence in Paradise could not be predetermined. This did not matter, since life was rooted in love. The sinner forfeits this openness. His time is circumscribed, and man starts calculating and defining everything, even God when he meets him again. It will take the coming of the Son and the founding of his Church in time to restore a genuine presence of the immeasurable Eternal in time. Until then there is only opposition; God in heaven, in his time and space which share in his immutability; we in our time and space that are now characterized by perishableness and death, a space and time outside Paradise where the eternal God used to walk in the time and space of the world.

A young person views the future as something desirable, and he tries to mature toward it. Whatever lies between the present and that point in the future which he has made his goal seems worth living for only insofar as he anticipates the attainment of the goal. As he grows older he learns to see more and more that things are perishable. Looking back on his life, he considers the past to be as important as, if not more important than, the present, to which he accords little intrinsic worth or relevance in his planning and acting. More vividly than before he recognizes the signs of weakness in himself and in his present moment. And people expect of him, as a mature person getting older, an ability to come to terms with perishableness, and an activity that makes sense within the flux of time.

But if he is a believer, then the changes in and around him, the growing sense of time passing, the inability to seize the moment and make it meaningful, all these must induce him to make room for the eternal in himself and in his environment. He must learn to live fully in the perishable world (without the comfort of a future) in order to become free and ready for eternity. For he cannot form his idea of the Eternal except with the help of a proper experience of life's passing nature, namely, with the help of his own relationship with God: of the image of God which faith permits him to construct in the gap between his being and the being of God, and of the time in which he lives and which becomes a symbol for him of the eternity which he will inhabit with God. And the more he concerns himself with the concept of perishableness, the more distinctly he experiences the passing of time and his inability to hold on to a particular hour, so much the more must he learn to shift his horizon of thought, faith and action from the perishable to the eternal. This shift must not lead to an imaginary existence in some impossible middle region between passing time and eternity; it remains strictly within perishable time but knows that its meaning and purpose are fulfilled in imperishable eternity. And while it is true that the believer receives insights into eternal truth and life through prayer, and is even actually transported into the world and milieu of God, nevertheless, on returning to his own world he cannot use this experience to deck out his earthly life with pretty images, as it were, in order to make it more livable. He should not try to fit eternity into the workaday world, but rather seek to open his daily life to the world of prayer and eternity in a spirit of readiness. If he is permitted to live simultaneously in both worlds, it is so that he may better understand and use the perishable world for having received insight into eternity; he should view this life as given by God to achieve maturity, eternity preparing him for eternity. Just as the Creator made the world and time without touching in the least the integrity of his eternal heaven, so the believer should begin to pray and live in dependence on eternity without violating this integrity—not trying to apply earthly categories to eternity, reducing and limiting it to the measure of his perishable days, but rather realizing the measure of his days as a parable given by God to introduce him into the reality of the eternal, where he will share fully in the vision and presence of God. Neither is the world to be changed through prayer and faith into an anticipated heaven; God's original intention was to create the world as something quite different from heaven. This is not to say that God withheld from the world whatever would make living in it desirable. It is the good environment of the good man. But according to the plan and the grace of redemption, the world was so broadly conceived at the start as to have a capacity for eternity.

If a Christian earnestly believes in the eternal God and knows him as Father, Son and Spirit, he also knows about the relations of love that exist among the Divine Persons from all eternity, relations of a totally divine character. By comparison, his own relations to his fellow men not only depend upon his particular state at any one time, but also suffer from the perishableness of external circumstances; they are not constant but subject to repeated vicissitudes beyond his control, which frequently take him by surprise. He may console himself with the thought that circumstances were against him, that his brother or spouse or friend was unfaithful for selfish reasons or simply by nature, while he, perhaps, would have remained faithful . . . had the other person only done so. But if he examines his relationship with God, he will have to admit that God is constant; he must ascribe to himself the vicissitudes in his relation to God. In the beginning was the Word, and this eternal Word is Love; it exists in heaven with God, and therefore remains simply Love, without diminution and without change. So perhaps man can best form a concept of eternity on the basis of the concept of love. Each time his relationship with God starts to vacillate, he must realize that he has been lacking in love, that he has not been faithful to the love of God and has treated it as a plaything of his moods. And so he must turn from himself and search elsewhere for the essence of love: he must contemplate the love between Father and Son in the Holy Spirit, that from the beginning was always the same divine love, that determines the entire relationship between the Persons and illumines and influences the entire atmosphere in which they live. They embody this love to such an extent that every being they encounter is drawn into it. If the essence of eternity can be deduced and explained above all from the fidelity and permanence of love, both concepts must be ordained to one another in their origin. In that case, eternity derives from love and leads back to it; it is an essential attribute of love. Love is characterized by steadfastness, which does not succumb to the passing of time but simply continues. A human being can give himself in love to another person; he can try to give him exquisite joy, try to live entirely for this love. Nevertheless, he will repeatedly grow weak and tired, turn away, even forget love altogether. In eternity there is no forgetting, because love is omnipresent, not as something incidental, but as the fundamental core of eternity. It simply cannot cease. It is a mutual exchange, like a ball tossed back and forth; it does not wear out, but rather continually guarantees new love and proofs of love. The guarantee lies not only in the fact that God is never disappointed in his love, but also in the fact that his love always seeks new objects and wider scope for itself. This love would remain only a vague theory for the believer if, along with its divine qualities, God had not imbued it with something that is comprehensible to man. Consequently, in comparing divine love to his human love, man can find in his own experience analogies to the intra-divine exchange between Father and Son. The believer knows love to be a gift that he receives, but also a gift that he gives; he knows its demands and sacrifices, and he is ready to accept certain privations, albeit imperfect and limited ones, so that the beloved may test the nature of his love. He realizes that his love grows stronger with every sacrifice and renunciation he makes. And so when he sees the Son of God becoming man to prove his love for the Father, and suffering even to death on the Cross, he cannot help but recognize therein a revelation of eternal love. And if he reflects on the magnitude of this sacrifice, if he seeks in prayer to grasp something of the sufferings of the Lord, he will also know that at best he can understand only a fraction of the real Passion which was the proof of the Son's love for the Father. Hence he must recognize that this love's true element is eternity. There is such force in divine love that it cannot confine itself to space and time. Seeing that the more this love extends itself into time, the stronger it appears, the Christian must conclude that it can be completely manifested only in eternity, eternity as the fruit of divine love, eternity in which the Son's sacrifice proves so fruitful that the triune God desires to open eternity to those whom the Son loved unto death, and for whose sins he died. Thus through the death of the Son eternity assumes for the believer both a present and a future quality, since it is there that he will experience the full power of divine love, by which he is borne now and beyond all time. He will experience it as one invited to partake of everything which wells up out of divine love and flows without end into eternity.

At creation the Father did not reveal his intentions regarding the ultimate union between heaven and earth. When, however, the Son becomes man and expounds in his own being the mysteries of the triune God to mankind, coming out of eternity and returning thither, man realizes God's purpose: to let him share in the same eternity to which the Son returns with him. The Son says Yes to all the works of the Father and to the Father's judgment that all the works are good; in becoming man he confirms to the Father how right he was and how wrong sinners were in trying to make the world into something different. And the Son does not wish simply to rescue souls from the world for heaven, but rather to take them there with the body which is destined for resurrection in order, through the redemption to consecrate for eternity everything that the Father created. So he will also take time into eternity—created time, manifold time, time that distinguishes and divides. He will gather up the days and nights into a mystery that belongs only to him. He will take with him everything that has made mankind happy here below according to God's purpose. Man will lack for nothing; rather, by becoming eternal, everything will be enhanced. This enhancement, rooted in love, will no longer be subject to decline and death but will enter into immortality.

Next to the love of the Son stands the mystery of the Church. When the Christian meets the Divine Persons from ever new aspects through reception of the sacraments and the course of the Church's year, and is led into constantly new mysteries of God and of his grace—while at the same time he sees in the feasts and ceremonies the reflection of his own perishable nature—everything becomes a sign that in heaven he will experience the fullness of the glorified Church and that this fullness will be imperishable, perfect and all-embracing. Through the fullness of the Church, the spotless Bride of the Lord, he is to receive the fullness of the vision of the triune God. While on earth, he must learn to interpret the passage of his own time as well as the events in the Church's year in such a way that he will become ready for the eternal liturgy in heaven. He should learn to recognize what is permanent in fleeting things. His faith, which he received as an indivisible unity and which his human vacillation cannot undermine, must be for him a sign of what is immovable, unchangeable: a sign erected on earth that is fulfilled in heaven. And through his faith he should experience the existence of what is unchangeable, and perceive it in God, in the saints in heaven and in the angels. All of them, present to him through his faith, will remind him of the eternal content of faith, thereby confirming and strengthening this content and causing it to develop and hold more than seemed possible.

When the Son on the Cross promises paradise in his company to the good thief, when he promises the future feast in heaven to the Apostles, when he speaks of the kingdom of his Father, he is always pointing toward eternity. However brief and close to the earth his words sound, they echo throughout infinite eternity and permeate the faith of his followers with their eternal content. He knows what he speaks of, what he brings with him and what he promises; and he can convey it to those who know it not. The very words he uses are designed to awaken in them a new sense: the sense of the eternal.

2

The Gate of the Church's Year

Confronted by the Lord's commandment of love, man is faced with a very remarkable question. He hears and understands the meaning of the words; he realizes that the issue is something so absolute that it is beyond him. In an instant he measures the distance between himself and the Lord, between his own capability and—by the standard of his capability—the unattainability of the commandment. But then he finds consolation in the notion of duration. It enables him to make a start, to press on with what is begun, to make at least some effort. The goal is to love his neighbor as himself. To attain this goal he must follow some path and needs time to envisage this path with his spiritual eyes and set out upon it. He needs, in other words, to have hope. If the time involved were a fixed term, if he could proceed step by step, eventually the moment would come when hope would break down and he would admit his defeat. And the time between resolution and disappointment would seem to be lost. At best he could only attempt the same procedure again, with renewed hope and good will, with a newly arranged system, only eventually to admit once more that he had failed. Each time, perishableness would overpower him in the collapse of his hopes.

The Lord gave his command as an absolute. But the believer knows that the Lord has set the goal in eternity, that he summons man to place this life in the service of the future life, to fashion his perishable time in view of the eternal time, to let his path lead into the Father's infinity. Relying on the future life, however, we must not grow careless and irresponsible. The Lord gave the commandment for the present time. He did not speak from heaven to give some vague direction, but spoke rather as a human being living among us. He came in order to bear the weight of our sins as a man; hence his human life is to be seen as a help to our keeping of the commandment. He gives us his life along with the commandment, not simply to skip over temporality, but to live with him in time in such a way that it receives an importance that the Father will not refuse to acknowledge. Struggle ensues from this union of his love with us. For him alone, without us, there would be no struggle, for he loves the Father and human beings; he *is* Love. We, however, are not-love, with which his love burdens itself in order to overcome it. This overcoming does not take place in eternity; the battle is fought on earth, unto the death on the Cross, within the measurable time of the Son's life that is depicted for us in Scripture, that we see as a limited period within our time, but that belongs so much to eternity that his years on earth cannot be subtracted from the eternity of the Son. Suffering in our time unto death, the Son makes known to us that the time of suffering is transitory, that his triumph in the Resurrection is a victory of heaven over earth, a proof of the Father's power in the Son of Man, and that we share in this victory and our present time will be conquered by imperishable time. The Son, therefore, puts his time—passing, yet replete with eternity—at our disposal in the Church as the Church's time, the Church's year, the Church's life, so that by living in it we shall share in Christ's own time.

Usually, a few dates of religious importance stick in a person's memory: perhaps recollections of First Communion or one's wedding day or ordination. A person may have felt himself absolutely committed to God and devoted himself earnestly to fulfilling this commitment, only to have to acknowledge now that the promise was not kept. Perhaps at that time he experienced his Yes as completely binding—perhaps as a child, in eager faith, he desired to become a priest. Today he is a married businessman who smiles over his lost enthusiasm and cannot really believe that he ever was so unworldly. Or perhaps he feels a faint compunction; he regrets that circumstances, the demands of life, his family, his own interests allowed him to forget the way of self-surrender he wanted to pursue. Or perhaps he has resolved in marriage and amid his professional duties to serve God better, to renounce certain pleasures; still he has slackened off, excusing himself on account of his weakness. Henceforth he will avoid such attempts in order to escape disappointment and not stray further from the path to God. Or perhaps he longs to be back in the days of his dedication and promises, and now tries to help others, his children for instance, to follow a really Christian way of life. And so he tells them what he had once planned and how much he has lost. Or perhaps he has actually become a priest; he is trying hard, feels the distance growing, but he does not despair and starts over again each day, learns greater humility through his defeats and does not look back to reckon up his earlier promises to God. Whatever the case may be, he always harbors religious memories. He knows that in the fleeting past he had experienced beginnings of a relationship with God; and he trusts in faith and prayer that the future will again bring such moments, enabling him to begin again in a new and better way. Such is the individual person's hope and hesitation before God.

But besides this experience, the Christian possesses something else: the Church's year, the life of the Lord, mirrored in the feasts of the Church and the quiet days that intervene. Between Christmas and Easter one contemplates the growing Son who lives in the presence of the Father, and one ponders his death; and from the Resurrection one's glance extends into the forty days, toward the Ascension and the mysteries of the Lord's indwelling in his Church. In between we celebrate the feasts of the saints: what they did and suffered and gave to the Church—countless ways of following the Lord and being faithful to him. The Christian looks forward to certain feasts that are particularly meaningful to him, and he suffers with the suffering Lord during the time of the Passion. Everything the Lord did and which is portrayed in the Church's year, all that is joyful and sorrowful has a personal meaning for him, imbues his own daily life, encourages him with new images of how to be a Christian, inspires his prayer, and as reality in the Church accompanies him and is as real and meaningful to him as the reality of his own life. Perhaps it is even more meaningful because it is a fuller reality, since there is no gap between the Lord's promise to the Father and its accomplishment; rather, he always accomplishes the Father's will in all his own desires, fulfills the Father's purposes in his own intentions, and enjoys the living vision of the Father in his prayer. And, contemplating the Lord, the Christian realizes what eternal life meant to the Son and what it means to the Church every day; he feels called to give eternity as much significance in his own life, and always to keep alive, through the days, the vision of imperishable eternity. He feels urged to offer his passing life, given him by God, in such a way that through grace it will become worthy to be received into eternal life.

Naturally, the believer can never place the reality of the Church's year simply on an equal footing with his own existence. Nevertheless, he can take something definite from his meditations on each feast and event of the Church's year and apply it to his own life. He will not be depressed over the failures in his own childhood when he reflects on the perfection of the Child Jesus or of the growing boy; rather, he will see therein the grace of a renewed invitation to the Church and to himself to say Yes to God each day in the same spirit of Christian childhood. Bathed in the light of the Christian feasts, everything takes on new illumination: the Christian's birthday, school, work; his difficulties, plans, decisions. This light that illumines everything is ecclesial, catholic and universal; it envelops what is private in the universal meaning of Christian existence in the Church and thereby emphasizes the importance of all that is individual, personal and ordinary. When the Christian stands with those who are dear to him before the mystery of Christmas, in meditating on the Holy Family he can gain encouragement for his own family and for himself as well; he will discover in himself a capacity, given to him in faith by God, to open the ancient mysteries from which generations of Christians have lived and been nourished, and to discover there a contemporary and personal meaning. It will be the same with all the mysteries of Christ, for all of them have the power to inspire his faith and give it new meaning and new direction. All of them are rich enough to bestow on him a perfectly unique experience each time, which as such will not pass away, but will last and endow his temporal existence with an eternal content. Externally the succession of the feasts corresponds with the course of the Christian's own life; at the beginning of the year he can see from the calendar on which days they will occur. And yet he knows in advance that it will not be the same Christmas, Easter or Pentecost as last year; new mysteries are waiting to be bestowed on him. It is impossible to be disappointed by any of the mysteries, or to be wearied by their recurrence; the power that the Lord brought to earth from eternity is so timeless and catholic that it can reveal as many new truths to today's Christian community and individual as to those in the past or in the future. The mysteries of God are so profound that they cannot be exhausted by any generation, not even by all of them put together; how much less by an individual somewhere in time!

The Christian should not only contemplate the mystery, but also make it his own, bringing it to blossom in his own being. In this process he may let his joy guide him wherever he feels drawn, provided that he never lose sight of the whole—the Church, catholicity. All things are interdependent, not diffusely and intangibly, but with the precision of a word specifically addressed to him; a challenge, a call, which as the word of God possesses the fullness of meaning. The Christian will also surround the sacraments and their reception with the spirit of the Church's year, conscious that both spheres, each with its own actuality, give life to each other; for example, meditation on the Risen Christ could culminate in Holy Communion at Easter, or confession could be made consciously bearing in mind the penitent or confessor whose feast is celebrated that day. In all of this he will keep in mind that the Church's year with its feasts and the sacraments which enrich Christian daily life have no other purpose than to remind him of and prepare him for the life that knows neither death nor sin, and that every mystery can be contemplated and integrated so as to point to the infinity of God. The Christian life with its days and years, each a different reminder of eternity, and the Church's year, with its constantly changing aspects that also point toward heaven, are woven together into a complex unity, in which each element has its designated place and which as a whole must become part of the unity of the Church of Christ. In contrast, eternal life appears to be the simple unity, taking all composite reality into itself—the Christian, the Church's year and the entire Church—in order no longer to allot them partial space and limited time, but rather to be itself—eternal space and eternal time for everything. Everyone invited into eternity may share in the whole. It is no longer the space created by God for man, but God's own space, into which he invites and receives created man. Eternal life cannot be grasped by the creature through the mere relinquishing of his fragmentary, divisible space and time: it is only eternal because it is divine life determined by the Divine Being. To regard it simply a continuation of earthly life would be to measure God by creaturely standards, or to see him as nothing more than a force that permeates the cosmos. What awaits us is

God's immeasurable nature: in the face of this, man loses his standard of measurement. This does not happen so that he might acquire another one in its place, but so that, by God's grace, he might live in his immeasurability in a fullness and boundlessness which is dependent on God and not on us, a world beyond our present comprehension. Earthly things are symbols and intimations; by the standards of eternal life, we are all still living in expectation. However great the leap is from the promise of the Old Testament to the fulfillment of the New, God intended it to be only a presentiment of what the leap from present time to eternal life will be. Through the grace of redemption much has been revealed to us that we can grasp in a fragmentary manner, but that even to the most advanced perception remains a parable until we see the Father face to face. This vision will replace everything else, will endow each eternal moment with a fullness that is derived from the vision and radiates from the triune God, so that meaning will be found only in him and not in ourselves. The Church, however, and catholicity, so important to us here, will have passed over into eternity in such a manner that her feasts and significant events will be absorbed into God's infinity, without disappearing in it. Just as they convey eternity in a concealed manner here and now and give us a presentiment of the presence and boundlessness of God, so on the other side they will possess it openly, and we will be permitted to use them as pointers in eternity to help us grasp the meaning of the eternal. Nothing that God gives during time will be lost in eternity, but everything that was distinct and analyzed on earth will be unified in heaven, without losing its character. We would never be able to enjoy the imperishable if we had not learned first in the perishable world to look forward to the imperishable.

3

The Gate of Faith

The Son, who took on our perishable time for the span of a human life, is God. As God he controls the eternal time in the vision of the Father, and fulfills our time with his time. For him too our time is fleeting—but in a different way than for us, because what he does and suffers in our time occurs before the face of the Father, and is directed toward him. The Father and the Son know the eternal character of the things he does in time and they remain united in this knowledge; his miracles and especially his words have an imperishable quality that human beings can sense. The power and urgency of his words are as strong today as if they were being uttered for the first time; they radiate eternal life.

And when the Son teaches us to pray, and puts into our mouth these words laden with eternal life so that we may repeat them after him, the words die away on our lips, yet they are still directed toward the eternal Father: each word is a bridge that stretches between our time and eternity. This can be proved true of each word, especially of the petition, "Thy will be done on earth as it is in heaven." "As it is in heaven" is an anticipation of our faith: the certitude that the Father's will is done in heaven, that eternity receives this will and that in eternity it is fulfilled, finding in eternity a time that is suitable to it. And now we offer our perishable time as a vessel to this same will, hoping that in our time it may find the same suitability. We expect—and the Son instills this expectation into us by teaching us his prayer—that our time may have an aptitude which is similar to eternity. And since the will of the Father is divine and eternal, and thus eternity, according to our expectation, can be reflected in our passing life, we may also expect that there is some point in the perishable world at which the eternal can hold fast forever. This takes place not only in the Son who adopted a temporal life, but also in our entire temporality, which can be totally taken over by the will of the Father to be its *locus* of action and development. It appears that God is thus subjected to what is perishable, but this is only an appearance, for he and his will are stronger than perishableness. When we pray the Our Father we are building a sound bridge, because the Son gives us the building stones, because the Son knows that the Father's will can be done on earth. And, in his visionary knowledge of the Father's will, he invites us to invite this same will to be done on earth, to offer the earth to the Father as a dwelling place. The Father created the earth and man; but we, as sinners, turned away from him. The Son invites us to return to the Father, and with us the whole earth: not just to promise as individuals to do his will, but as parts of the whole, the earth. The Son created a visible organization in the Church, to stand before the Father as a symbol for the whole world. And thus we invite the Father to do his will in the Church, and to do it in us, since we are members of the Church. It is a thoroughly catholic invitation because it includes the individual as well as the universality. All living things—the Church as well as the individual Christian—are to become a dwelling for the Father, a dwelling for the imperishable will of God in the midst of perishable time.

Not only this petition of the Our Father, but every prayer contains such a sign of the power of God on earth. It is a dialogue between a conceivable reality (the individual Christian or the Church as a whole) and someone who is inconceivable, who infinitely exceeds our understanding, yet who in some way does correspond to our idea, since we know through the Son that he hears and acts and that his time intervenes in our time. But God does not intend to let his eternity penetrate our time in such a way that we would recognize it everywhere by our own powers. It retains its superiority as that which existed long before we came into being; it withdraws from our grasp which would pin it down and remains for us the Other, the Divine, heaven. Thus it remains for us a superior state of being precisely because it escapes our grasp, because neither our experience nor our faith can find a name for it. It is always we who are grasped, even when we think we have grasped something. Eternity holds us in contemplation, while it is action: more active, more effective than our time, though in faith it offers our time the possibility to perceive it and to surrender to it, the possibility for time to perceive itself as a function of eternity ordained by God.

If we tried in our faith to define exhaustively all its contents here below, we should find ourselves setting the boundaries proper to human concepts, and finally everything would be topsy-turvy: eternity would be viewed as a function of perishable time. But if we try to remain in a believing, open surrender, we will understand that it is we who are defined as those who are created, who remain in the function of the Creator. Out of eternal time our time receives the rays of grace sent by God; we may understand these rays as the signs of his existence, and, persevering in prayer and hope, we may receive these rays as pledges of

God's favor. God's time overarches our time. We need not understand every ray as God does; it suffices if each one that reaches us remains a sign of his vitality, granted to us in order to be experienced in the sign of that same divine vitality. Each time it is like a breath from God stirring the surface of the waters of our existence, giving more meaning to our life, more fullness to our time.

Sin taught us to calculate and to measure, to accumulate passing things in order to survive the risk of existence and to determine the portion allotted to each mortal. It is not enough to establish what is mine and thine; both have to be weighed within time and the changeableness proper to each, because time and circumstances change, and we change likewise. Consequently, we are uncertain about our own life and that which pertains to it. Faith alters the balance: everything that is good belongs to God, and we serve him by administering the good things he offers us according to his will. God's standards of measurement for us are not ours, and we are afraid of his standards. We are afraid to allow God complete freedom. We cannot get rid of our tendency to measure things, and always fall back on measuring other people and comparing our experiences with theirs. In this connection the Incarnation of God takes on new meaning for us. The Son lived inconspicuously among us; those meeting him must have been inclined to apply to him the same norms as those applied to other people. But they had to admit their mistake; his words had a background that others' words did not have, they revealed mysteries clad in human words that remained incomprehensible to the measuring listener and were clear only to the person who, in faith, forgot all measurement. The Son lived adapted to the framework of our time: his days passed like ours, his needs seemed to be the same as ours, and he divided his time the same as we do. At the same time he spoke continually about things that were not of this world and yet were his. It must have been embarrassing for his companions to have to give up the usual categories because the Son did not accept them and did not use them in his replies, but rather spoke and lived in a different time which was perfectly real to him but incomprehensible to them. Since then the Church has had time to contemplate his words and to present them to us in such a way that we are less tempted to apply our own standards to him; rather, since the Lord no longer speaks as a man on earth, we can hear his voice as that of eternity. All the situations and circumstances in the Son's life indicate one truth: that eternal life was much more important, decisive and urgent for him than temporal life. Everything about him was a reminder to put our own time at the disposal of eternal time. Not only does he speak of eternal things; his very being withdraws him again and again from our comprehension. He speaks about the Father, saying he is one with him; he ascends to heaven and from there sends the Holy Spirit. The man who has anything to do with him meets God in three Persons. In the Church of today, we are no longer confronted with his appearance in the flesh. We cannot apply the standards that for a moment were useful to his contemporaries (for they were human standards and fulfilled their function by palpably demonstrating their futility), because we are confronted from the outset with the spiritual Son, as one of the Three, although we have never encountered a three-personal being in this world. But it is precisely through this threefold being of the eternal that the time out of which Christ speaks takes on new dimensions for us that are wholly foreign to our created time. We can only submit to them in faith and be open to them by endeavoring to do the will of the Father. And we do this when we receive his Word as the Son, acknowledge it as *the* fulfillment of the Father's will on earth as it is in heaven, and therefore place our time at the disposal of eternal time; accepting, in other words, the contrast between our circumscribed system and the immensity of God through an act of faith which is completely devoid of any wish to measure, so that finally our knowledge is submerged in our faith, the center of which is the divine knowledge of the Son.

The word of the Son is always a demand. He makes demands on himself, as he recognizes in his own words the goal of his earthly existence. In the fulfillment that he personifies he sees contained the call to fulfill his task. He wants to save the world; he will do it through himself, the Word of the Father. But the words that he speaks and that express himself and his teaching have a preeminent place in his work because they reveal to men the truth according to which they must live, the meaning of their existence. The word, therefore, is also a demand upon the man who receives it: he must act according to it and grow into it in order to become the person that the Father, through the Son, requires. This demand does not place man in a vacuum; it is surrounded by a grace that helps him toward its fulfillment. Thus the demand is both the goal and the path: the goal is contained in the word of eternal life, but the path to eternal life is the word. God gave to the first man a woman to be his counterpart, but they sinned together. Then God gave man a new, surpassing companion—his Son. He permitted the Son to humble himself so far as to become a man and to encounter other human beings. But since he is continually returning to the Father, he does not cease to be one of the Divine Persons and therefore uses all the divine means to prepare those whom he meets for eternal life: by means of himself, his surrender, his readiness to do the Father's will and to bring the world back to God. Eternal life is contained in the Son; he embodies it, not as a foreign element, but rather he bestows it as his own. First and foremost he bestows it in the word. The word becomes the pledge of eternal life. Each of his words contains it, carries it and bestows it, drawing the recipient into itself: into the Son, and through the Son into God's triune life. The word is spoken here and now, in historical time, yet as such it loses nothing of its divinity; it strikes home, forms, educates and guides with divine efficacy. And even though the Son no longer lives visibly on earth, his word lives on in the Church with the same immediacy. She bears it, makes it perceptible and bestows it, not as mere word, but in connection with the Son's sacramental miracles; word and sacrament combine to form an indissoluble, undivided truth, which is always flowing into the eternal life of the

Son. It is inconceivable that a word of the Son could be uttered into human perishableness so as to adopt and assume this quality. The most temporal word of the Son always transcends time, and the most topical is always eternal; the moment of its utterance endures forever. Thus the word of itself signifies eternal life: as Word-Son, but also as the word spoken and given. And if we try to see his entire divine-human being in every word spoken by the Son, the unity of his being as the Word of the Father and his spoken word will become clearer and clearer. Nowhere in this unity can we detect a hiatus, a flaw. We understand that his being the Word of the Father indicates the mission of the Son, the purpose of which is to lead the perishable world back to the eternal one. And if we adore the Word, contemplating it and building our life in faith upon it, because it is no longer we who live, but Christ who lives in us, we will be educated by the word and made mature for eternal life.

When a man loves someone else—his wife or child—he knows that his love is subject to the conditions and demands of earthly life and will be affected by the laws of perishableness. He may wish his love to endure forever, but he is powerless with regard to the length of life accorded to him or to his beloved. He can enhance only the content of time, never the vessel. Neither can he protect either of them against attacks from without—unforeseen harm, illnesses and death. Nor does he know whether the love of the other person will be constant, whether his own love can become the rule of life for the beloved, whether he or she will not find someone who is more worthy of love. Uncertainty is the companion of his love. The step between being loved and being rejected is small. For this reason he endeavors to make his love as creative as possible, in order to keep the other's love awake.

But when as a Christian he begins to love the Lord, he suddenly finds himself face to face with a quite different love—a love that is constant, imperishable, and which the Lord will never disavow. There is no fear of a possible rejection; any infidelity can only be one's own. And so the Christian exposes himself to this eternal love, lets himself be loved in order to learn how to love. If his love is inventive and seeks for intensification and better proofs, he knows that no love is more inventive than the Lord's and that he could find no better proofs than those offered by the Lord, that his own love could never be more fruitful than when fructified by the Lord, and thus that in order to become a giver he must above all be a receiver. When, at the beginning, he comes up against certain limits, he will have to admit that he himself, and not the Lord, put them there; that he has erected them out of the imperfection of his love for the Lord, out of a human desire for security, to avoid falling at once into the limitless and being overcome by the vertigo of infinity. But if he lets the Lord help him remove these limits, he gradually understands that the divine love which loves him remains beyond his understanding and that in every encounter with the Lord he meets something of eternal life. The infinity of the Lord's love becomes for him a mirror of eternal life. Here on earth the Christian experiences something of eternal life in the love of the Lord. He no longer uses his reason and his pitifully small love as a measure; rather, he will let the Lord's love lead him into the heart of this love. The Lord will signify the eternal to him, and his own perishable state will appear as a covering which he will be glad to be allowed to shed, in order to stand naked in the nakedness of the eternal. Hesitant, he still tries to cover himself up, creating obstacles between himself and the Lord; however great his surrender and the dedication of his earthly life, he cannot achieve the ultimate unveiling; he must long for eternity, where the total truth of the Son and the complete vision of the triune life will be given to him. In no way can he determine how far he still is from this unveiled Love (possibly because there are no measurable distances), but he knows that death is the entrance and that this gate leads through the life of the Son.

4

The Gate of the Sacraments

Through his Incarnation the Son established in himself an uninterrupted union between heaven and earth. On earth he was the mirror of what goes on in heaven. And since he gave his whole life to man without reserve, man partakes in a certain measure in this mirroring of heaven. And since he is entirely one of us, this mirror is among us so that all who come into contact with him in any way experience something of the life of heaven. In becoming man the Son did not step out of his center: as man he remains the center of heaven and precisely thus becomes the center of the world. And since God the Father never takes back any of his gifts, so nothing in revelation was terminated with the Ascension of the Son: the Father and the Spirit remain what they are, and the Son remains the Savior of the world in his surrender to the Father, and so the openness of heaven to earth which was brought about through the Incarnation remains too. The Son returns to heaven, but it does not close after him. Grace loses nothing of its reality and presence. Living signs of heaven remain behind on earth. These signs are found not only in the answer to all prayers made in his name, an answer based on the Son's personal contact with the faithful on earth and the triune God in heaven—a contact which, from God's point of view, is objective and constant, while in the person praying (eagerly or haltingly) it always has a subjective side to it. The Lord also leaves with the Church the sacraments as a sign of the living presence of heaven on earth, as a pledge that loses nothing of its freshness and immediacy. The Church was instituted for all time, and while during the course of history new people continually flock to her, still all generations encounter this never-waning relevance of eternal life: the sacraments instituted by the Lord himself.

Baptism elevates man to the state of grace; through the vitality of the Church he shares in the vitality of the Son and in the gifts of the Holy Spirit. He is washed, changed, born anew and his spirit receives a disposition toward God. He is not baptized into future, temporal life, but into eternal life. The prayers and ceremonies of baptism—being breathed upon, being sealed with the sign of the Cross, being washed and anointed—are all examples of the opening of heaven and the pouring out of a life that is not of this world, yet flows into it in order to create a living connection with heaven, in order to place a mark upon the baptized by which the Father can recognize that he belongs to the Son, a sign of a continuing membership, of a condition that cannot be revoked. The seal is indelible. No apostasy from God has the power to wipe it out. Man may want to forget this grace; but it will never forget him. The Church is always the place where this connection is effected and made known; through each baptism the Church receives an increase in grace, which cannot be taken from her even through the defection of the baptized person. One can deprive the Church of attributes appropriate to her, but they are not located where the Church reaches up into heaven: her relationship to God would remain the same if only one member remained faithful.

Nothing seems to happen, to the eyes of the unbeliever, when bread and wine are changed into the Body and Blood of Christ. The mystery revealed by heaven in the Eucharist is given only to faith. However, the faith of the individual present at the Consecration through the mediatorship of the Church is not the cause of the Consecration; rather, the office of the Church is the cause, in which an immediate union between heaven and earth is established. In this way Consecration differs from Communion: Consecration is a mystery of the Lord given to the Church, which occurs through the office, without the celebrant's faith adding to it. Indeed, he would not be there if he did not believe. But if he had lost his faith, the Consecration would occur just the same. The inviolable relation between heaven and earth in the Eucharist is not placed in the hands of the individual believer. As certainly as the natural intellect can depend on the operation of the law of gravity under given conditions, so certainly the miracle of Consecration takes place for the Church: not on the grounds of the Church's faith, but of the Lord's promise made thousands of years ago. As man he promised, and from heaven he keeps his promise; it is and remains his gift. But he would not give it if the Church did not possess throughout time the faith through which she remains perpetually open and in communion with heaven. The Lord bestows upon this faith his Body, which has the power to transform the recipients and to work in them as eternal life. His Body lives in them with the same vitality and certainty as the Son lived among men in his life on earth. Actually, he has only gone one step further: at that time he lived among us; now he lives in us. He has transposed the mystery of his Incarnation into each individual believer. And he works from within each one, for into each he has placed the mirror of heaven by means of Communion. This new life does not plunge the Christian into doubts and questions, into a burdensome fate; rather, it is the radiant and striking presence of the Lord in him—today and forever. A mirror of heaven sparkles at one point in the world, undiminished, uncompromising and endowed with the strength to transform man and his whole activity toward heaven.

Before the Ascension the Son promises to send the Holy Spirit. Having instituted the Eucharist, he now takes his leave and completes the movement back to heaven, while through his return the Spirit accomplishes the reverse movement. And since both of them are God, the Trinity in Unity is made manifest to the faithful: the Father remains in heaven; the Son returns to the Father; the Spirit is sent by the Son from heaven. All three statements combine to open heaven for the believer—a heaven of movement, of triune life, a heaven that could not have been given more obviously than in this threefold manner of remaining, going and coming. The Son disappears from the sight of his followers into eternity, while the Spirit suddenly descends upon them from the same eternal life in flames, in a tumult in which a new world is plunged into the existing one. Those struck by the Spirit can speak in tongues and in new languages and make themselves understood in this turbulence, which to unbelievers appears as only confusion, with words they did not know before. They are so full of the Spirit that their whole being and action overflow with it, and they represent to others something totally unique: existence in a world to which entrance is gained only by the Spirit. It is a new opening of heaven, without distance, since those affected surmount their normal human limitations: the limits of the spirit are overcome in the Spirit. For the Holy Spirit has chosen their spirit as his dwelling and given it laws that are no longer the laws of this world. For the moment they are released from the burden of seeking, learning and acquiring; they are freely granted that which they can only receive gratis, through grace: a new, expanding, strange life, that does not submit to their finiteness. It is a surprise attack on man, especially the believer who thought he could manage his own faith, but now realizes that faith is not some quality that accompanies him through life, but a force coming directly from heaven, from the triune God. The Son's going to heaven expands into the Spirit's coming from heaven. And meanwhile the Father does not cease to send the Son, nor Father and Son together to send forth the Spirit; and so the faith bestowed on man remains in constant touch with the threefold vitality of God in heaven. Faith is the pledge of the infinite reality of God in eternity but equally the pledge to earth of the reality of heaven, of heaven's being poured out upon it, causing it to share totally in this new and other reality. The visible sign of this change in the faithful through the Spirit is confirmation, a sign that must become action in them. The work accomplished in them by the Spirit is symbolized by the speaking in tongues, but continues in their daily life. In the first assault of the Spirit this new ability appeared in a unique and striking manner, but it left behind something permanent—a new capacity of perception. Just as the disciples recognized at Pentecost that the Lord was keeping his promise, so those receiving confirmation are empowered to recognize the revelations of the Spirit. They know him as the One who has visited them, and they can recognize him again. They will recognize him in others as well as in themselves as the power exerted not once and for all, but permanently at the service of all the living impulses from heaven, opening new ways which are of heavenly origin, and yet are revealed to lead to Christian ways on earth. In this manner, the new strength grows into one of profession, of responsibility, demanding testimony from the confirmed: they must bear witness, not only to what has happened to them and to the other faithful, but also to whatever the Spirit may do. It is the testimony, not of weak, sinful man with his flickering faith, but of the Spirit acting in the fullness of power within him.

The Son, who at his parting promised the Spirit, also instituted the sacrament of confession. It was established by him as the official forgiveness of sins. He begot it on the Cross in torment; it will be fulfilled in his Spirit. And it is related to the sacrament instituted at Pentecost, which refers to it. Man can bear witness to himself and to God. He bears witness to himself in the confession of his sins before the forgiving God, while everything that occurs in confession and after it is a witness to God, a declaration of the Holy Spirit about him. This declaration even gives form to man's confession of sin. For whatever man tells about himself, with the exception of his naked sins—concerning his return to God, his turning away from evil—is not merely talk about himself, but more truly about the work of God within him. And if he were to lose sight of this work, no matter what he might say of himself, it would be useless and pointless and would have nothing to do with the sacrament. Confession and the descent of the Spirit are so intimately connected because the one absolved is not placed in a vacuum, but rather in the fullness of the Spirit. The Spirit of the office gives him absolution and enables him to know in a new and free manner and to act in his name, and to do in the truth of the Spirit what he formerly neglected through sin. Confession is not simply a negative cancellation of sin, but rather from the outset an openness to confirmation, to the positive reception of the Spirit and to perseverance in him. Confession of sin is a way to the Spirit, is already part and parcel of the Spirit, because contrition is already a harbinger of his presence and the beginning of a new orientation through the working of the Spirit, who becomes completely manifest in the priest's exhortation and absolution. The penitent recognizes the Spirit working in the confessor when the latter gives the exhortation; and in the absolution the Spirit shows his power at work, through the confessor, in the penitent. And since the Spirit comes from heaven bearing witness to eternal life and manifesting the triune God, the penitent encounters eternal life each time as the promise that God wishes to fulfill in him. The Son's suffering on the Cross went as far as abandonment by God, the descent into hell; but from there his path turns sharply in the direction of heaven. This same turning occurs at the conclusion of confession. It is true, the sinner has already repented according to God's plan, but his confession is like a path proposed through his own hell, past his piled-up sins; and suddenly this path ends in the brightest light of grace. In rising, the Son made himself the object of heaven's power, the eternal power of the infinite Father, who leads him from death to life. The penitent comes out of hell, to the horrors of which he has contributed through his sins; suddenly he is plunged into a resplendence that is not of this world, heaven's cascading ocean of light in which eternal life is revealed to him. It is a shock, without transition: he who was condemned to hell for his sins awakens amid eternal grace. Perhaps through repeated reception of the sacrament one's perception can be dulled. But as long as faith remains alive the Christian is bound to experience this miracle, of which he has objective knowledge, as a new beginning. He has been placed in a world that is new to him, where he can experience new things through the newly received Spirit. No absolution is simply a repetition of a previous one, for each time a part of heaven is opened in an unexpected manner. If the Christian were more conscious of this perception through the spirit of absolution, if he took it more deeply into his prayer life, he could live from it in an entirely fresh certainty, could make entirely fresh decisions and use resources that are available but otherwise remain hidden in the power of the Spirit. That in which he partakes is not evoked through his deliberations, studies or self-scrutiny; rather, it is already given in the excess of grace flowing to him from heaven, grace that shatters the limitations of his deliberation and action through its creativity, which stems from eternity. He shares above all in mysteries of discipleship, of service, of unconditional dedication, which, in being bestowed in this manner—not without a veil, yet revealed as new and different—demonstrate their reality and feasibility in God, in whom they were always hidden and taken up. And so, being seized by the Holy Spirit, he is really being seized by the omniscience and the providence of God. The person who follows God's ways can leave behind the earthly way of looking at things; he can regard the whole scheme of redemption—that paramount truth—as placed at his disposal, and he can act according to the laws of eternity, even when these laws for the time being seem inscrutable. He surrenders to Providence, without wishing to command it.

The sacraments, instituted by the Lord as man and given to the Church, were tested by him on earth: each in its own way. He knows what is meant by giving one's body; what it means to institute the Eucharist as a continuation of his earthly existence in a form accessible to human beings. He knows what it means to go through hell after having borne the weight of the sin of all mankind. On the Cross he actively suffered the actual sins of each individual and experienced them subjectively, somehow encountering them fully and personally. In the underworld, in the alienation of death, he saw sin in its pure objectivity, no longer as something tangible to be borne, but with insight into that which is discarded and remains on the refuse heap. For this reason he gives to the sacrament of penance a double character: first, the personal confession and consciousness of subjectivity, of having committed these and not other sins; second, the sharing in the sin of the whole world, which is illimitable, but not for that reason any less real. Every penitent undergoes not only the Cross but in an indefinable fashion the underworld as well, even if he is totally unaware of it. In this way, absolution too gains a double force: in one sense the Christian receives grace for himself personally, according to his personal confession; in another sense, he receives it as a grace to be shared, belonging to the Church, as a response to his objective sharing in every sin of the world. He receives from eternal life something that is always somehow discernible, but also something that is totally undiscernible, that is destined above and beyond him for others. In every sacramental bestowal of eternal life there are these personal and general elements—that which is destined for the individual in the Church and that which is destined for the Church in general —and the latter may be intended, in turn, for other particular individuals. We see, therefore, that the sacramental life, as a turning of heaven toward earth, an opening of many doors into eternity, and a form for the participation of Christian life in the life of the Lord, is always both personal and ecclesial.

5

The Gate of Ordination and the Consecrated Life

In the relations of the Divine Persons there is a constancy that is grounded in the Father and is communicated to the Son and the Spirit, guaranteeing absolutely the place and relation of each Person. They share something of this with the believer out of their eternal life, but it can only be understood in the context of the Church founded by the Son. One of the purposes of the Church is to reveal in herself concretely something of the life of God in eternity. It would not do for Christians to have only a blurred idea of eternal life as something limitless and unimaginably great, leaving it up to the individual to give it content and outline according to his own mind and imagination. The Church presents us with the infinite life of God in a valid form that can become intelligible to us in faith. She does not do this by adapting to our own ideas of life, but by revealing a mysterious divine life within her, visible in her structure. Individual Christians, each according to his vocation, may develop these lines for themselves, but only insofar as the emerging image does not contradict the image arrived at by other Christians.

In order to safeguard God's revelation from being distorted by men during the course of time, the Son founded the Church and within it the office of priesthood, whose task it is to administer revelation officially and hand it on in a suprapersonal validity guaranteed by the Lord. Certainly there will be individual occurrences within the tradition that will surpass the usual form: theologians of rank who through their researches open up new perspectives; private revelations, surprising discoveries and a widening of understanding; but all these prove their genuineness in the fact that they can, in the end, be ordered into the continuity. What at first seems totally new, even disruptive, and cannot be mathematically deduced, will still, when rightly formulated, find the place reserved for it in tradition and be woven together with related truths and integrate itself organically into the age-old teachings. Discoveries in moral or speculative theology prove to be fruitful for prayer, renew the love of neighbor, awaken new forms of religious life and give to priests new tasks in charity. In all this the pastoral office retains its immutable responsibility of apportioning and accepting these new forms of spiritual life. It is what stands firm in the flowing movement of the Church's vitality, shaping both the Church and the individual office-bearer.

When a young man decides to consecrate himself entirely to God, he is ready to be obedient to all that God may plan to do with him in the Church. He lets himself be tested and taught and shaped like wax in the Church's hand. For he knows of the mystery between Christ and the Church, the fruitfulness between Bridegroom and Bride. He is drawn into their mystery, so that he himself can count on one day bearing fruit in the service of the Lord. Whatever happens to him during his development occurs in the name of the Lord's love for his Church, to help her increase on earth. The more he is drawn into the mystery of the Church's fruitfulness, however, the more thoroughly he will lose sight of his own fruitfulness. He leaves this to the great order, which is beyond him. When he is ordained priest a further change occurs: he is drawn into a state that is purest objectivity and therefore corresponds neither to his subjective hopes nor to the objective expectations he had as a believer. For the office in which he now receives a share is not comprehensible to faith; in its essence it derives from the mystery of God, from eternal life. While a young seminarian, he said Yes to God with his whole personality. Now at ordination his surrender takes on a new form. It is as if he must put on a ready-made garment, the measurements of which apparently have no bearing on his own figure. What he has to represent from now on is more the garment than himself, a cause demanding his service; what he is to administer are the already existing sacraments, and what he is to preach is the word of the Church. This is a second adaptation. At the beginning of his career he was drawn by the Bridegroom (to whom he had given his assent) into the spirit of the Church-Bride; now he must once more enter the mystery between them, in order to know and see the Bridegroom better from the position of the Bride. And if now the question arises of his individual wishes, the enrichment of his personality, the use of his talents, there can be no other answer than the disclosure of his inessential place within the essential relationship between God and the Church. He stands at the point where the Church becomes fruitful through God; from the Church, with complete respect and attention, he is to accept rule of life, form, tradition, Scripture, and from the Lord he is to receive the personal message of the word, the responsibility for his personal task and for the fulfillment of his mission. He must let his most subjective being as a Christian be permeated by the utter objectivity of the Church, so that both may ripen to fruition in him. He is both supernumerary—not counted as a person; he belongs to the priestly office—and indispensable, because God has called *him* to this office and asks him to fulfill his personal vocation within this prescribed framework. He is trapped right from the beginning of his priestly existence. It is his task to represent the Lord in his earthly life, to affirm everything that he affirmed on earth, in perpetual fidelity to accept everything that can happen to a Christian on earth and to do so in the name of the Lord in heaven, to conceive of his life as entirely under the direction of the Lord, and thus to become an embodiment of the Church. But the Church and her ministry cannot be understood, any more than the earthly life of the Lord (which she continues), without his heavenly life. Just as the life of the Son, for a given number of years, was the presence of eternity within time, so the priest also lives as a man in the perishable order, but as one who bears office he represents a penetration of eternity into time. In his official capacity, he cannot utter a word or perform an action or administer a sacrament that would not be most closely connected with what transpires and has validity in heaven. He is the daily representation (often oppressively so) of what occurs in its fullness in heaven; he is the mission to manifest eternal life in Church life; he is the obligation always to let the eternal meaning of God radiate from the events of daily life. If anyone asks, "What is God doing today?" the answer would be: "He is doing what he has done from all eternity without interruption, and what is today as urgent and personal as ever: he is begetting his Son." In like manner, what the priest does is always ecclesial, as it was from the beginning of the Church and will be as long as she exists. And yet what he does is his personal mission, contemporary and vital.

If the priest in his ministry stands between the Church and the Son—and that means at the heart of the Church, for her center is not within herself, but at the point where she exchanges her life with the Lord—the religious is a step closer to the Lord: by definition he is placed in the closest imitation of Christ, on the Cross. This does not mean that he can occupy the place of the Cross himself, but that his whole life consists of elements of the Cross. He approaches the Cross through his readiness to accept whatever the Lord sends him of his own destiny, and this is none other than to save the world, something which cannot be accomplished except on the Cross. In this manner the Cross is erected in the life of the religious. This situates him at the very place where the Crucified gives his Mother to the disciple, commits his Bride to the Church's love, hands over his Church to the one who will bring her to fulfillment. Henceforth love and suffering are part of the legacy of the Church, entrusted to the religious in a special way. In his life there is a twofold movement: toward the Cross and from the Cross. In his obedience he will constantly keep his eyes focused on the obedience of the Lord who goes to meet the Cross. He accompanies him from the Mount of Olives to the Resurrection; in the middle of the path stands Golgotha. In the life of a priest the place assigned to him may be located somewhere in the public life of the Lord where the Cross is only a presentiment. And, whereas the priest experiences again and again the tension between ecclesial office and his own personality, the personality of the religious is immersed from the start in that of the Lord, who came to save the world through suffering. His prayer flows into the Son's will to obey the Father; his wishes and expectations merge with the Lord's expectations in regard to the Cross. When he pronounces his vows, he becomes one of the countless number who promise discipleship; at the same time he is the special one in whom the Father recognizes the mark of his Son. His abilities are used under obedience, and he is permitted no other wish than to be a disciple. By doing so he certainly does not presume to live up to the divine demand; but he may not relax his absolute striving toward that goal and must accept through his superiors the will of God in an attitude of perseverance and wisdom, which alone will enable him to understand what God requires of him. This firm structure within the order and within the obedience it imposes is already the Cross for him, all the more so because in this structure and in the persons placed over him he will not always feel the presence of God, just as the Son on the Cross no longer felt the presence of the Father.

The Son, who promises the Redemption to the Father, is able as God to survey the magnitude of his sacrifice. As man he promises the Father obedience and fidelity, without placing any limits on what he has promised. He does not say how far he will go, how long he will endure this life, how often he will give of himself in preaching and working miracles. In making his promise, he is prodigal in generosity to the Father as he will be prodigal for us on the Cross. It is a case of "beyond measure", both in heaven and on earth. This earthly extreme can be grasped only by the faith that opens itself as far as possible in order to receive the immeasurable heavenly superabundance as a living reality. This is where the religious shares in eternal life. Within this openness he discovers the material of his vows, the substance which springs from the Yes of the Son and is interpreted in a human way in the Yes of his Mother. Mary's assent to the angel occupies a kind of middle place between the heavenly Yes of the Son and its fulfillment on the Cross; it indicates the extremity of a human being's capacity for surrender. And when Mary is given into John's keeping, her extreme response is confirmed, justified and receives the promises of heaven. For the religious, the Mother's adoption at the foot of the Cross is a guarantee.

When the Father sends forth his Son and promises the redemption of all creation as the reward of his pains, his intention is to let the new reality which the Son will bring from heaven to earth continue unhindered, in the continual transformation of each individual life offered to the Lord for his purposes. The Son is the sower; persons under vows are the seed, destined for further sowing, which in springing up shares the fruitfulness that the Father has designed for the Son's seed. This seed so flourishes that its fruit cannot be measured. It is the sprouting of heavenly reality on earth, whose fruits, because they are heavenly, cannot be predetermined. The official, priestly Church presses toward shape and formulation, trying to leave as few gaps as possible. Religious life, on the contrary, continually permits new things to spring up in the midst of what has been established; it is so turned toward heaven and open to it that even the most stringent rules cannot calculate or capture in advance what the ultimate fruits will be. The field of achievement is so extensive that most of it escapes survey and remains hidden in eternal life with the Father. The image of eternal life is different from the viewpoint of religious life than it is from the viewpoint of ecclesial office. The office *sees* merit and the classification of human accomplishment which can be expressed in words. It is obliged to do this because it is catholic and must reckon with all humanity. Here the element of that which is ever greater and ever expanding occurs in the sacraments. For the religious, however, rules and the measurement of achievement disappear, because what his existence expresses is a truth of eternal life that can be grasped only through prayer. This truth is in the Church and extends throughout time, but it remains intangible, as all heavenly things escape the grasp of earth as long as the second coming of the Lord is not a present reality. One can even say that the official Church lives with an eye on the judgment, while the Church of the vows lives by the parousia. Or more exactly: from the Cross in respect to all things earthly and from the parousia in respect to all things heavenly; earthly life from the Cross, the life of prayer from the parousia. And the overall attitude is suspension between Cross and parousia.

The Lord has said: "No one comes to the Father except through me." The Father is seen here both as the essence of the eternal, triune life and the goal of the Christian way. The Son is the way and the gate leading to it; and the way implies a going, a walking. When, however, priests and religious—those persons in the Church who are placed in a special relation to Christ as gate and way and to heaven as eternal life—when these persons receive a share in this path-like quality which is shared by Christ and the Church, it is never for their own private advantage. Instead, they are to demonstrate to Christians and to all the world the necessity of the way, and this in a twofold sense: they are to let genuine eternal life pour into the world through the sacraments and the word of God; and in being fully convinced of the value of what they do, they will receive through grace the ability to clothe in words what has been wrought, known and believed; and these words, not being clichés, will convince others. But they must not only point the way; they must also lead. The power to do so lies in what they themselves are: those who are led and become leaders, those moving along the way who cause a movement. It is useless to point to heaven as a place to be desired, to praise the blessedness of God in eternal life or to present to mankind the necessity of the way thither—if those who do the talking are not going there themselves. No one will feel compelled to begin the journey of his own accord. Those commissioned by the Lord must be mediators in their entire existence: mediators of what they possess and what they are striving for. Certainly they cannot be perfect. But they must cling so much to what is perfect that their difference from others will be conspicuous and people will desire access to the mysteries and miracles that are open to them. When mundane daily existence is full of conflict or perhaps full of boredom, man finds it difficult to imagine a hereafter; he does not know the harmony of eternity. Perhaps he confuses it with his own boredom, or he expects tensions in heaven similar to those known on earth. But when people who are called by God's grace to have genuine knowledge of heaven and the life of the Blessed Trinity live a genuine heavenly life on earth in the presence of their fellow human beings, then the sacramental actions and divine words, the sermons and prayers, the works of charity will point much more clearly to a fulfillment in heaven. When the way to heaven is lived out in a credible manner, the goal, heaven itself, will become desirable to all those who see it. And this pointer toward heaven will not be like a boring moral tract; rather, because it is a lived life, it will itself beget life: it will bring heavenly life close to people and fill human life with the mysteries of God, making it richer, more pliant and more obedient to him.

The praise of God for which man was created is often difficult for him in this life. And the Church's words, intended to set before him the meaning of his life, are often so worn out that they are scarcely heard at all. We need persons who will pour the original power into these words, directly from eternal life, so that the words will rejoice the hearts of those who praise the Lord, because they flow fresh from the treasures of him who is praised; but also so that the words will show the Father how much the Son is loved on earth, and the Son how much the Father and the Spirit are loved. The words of praise create a relationship to the eternal God that does not stray into uncertainty, but rather gives proof of the knowledge that God bestows, of the service that man gives, of the love that unites heaven and earth. Priests and religious must not only testify to what they know; they must be this testimony themselves. This is difficult, but it is the fruitfulness that brings man close to God: God walking on earth and God in the eternal life of heaven. When someone sees that a person is leaving everything to follow the way to eternal life—a way of poverty with the God who became poor, a way of prayer, a way, too, of riches from the treasure-house of God's love—then no spoken word can surpass in power this word that is lived.

6

The Gate of Prayer

Through the voice of the prophets in the Old Covenant man already discovers how much God is concerned with him, desiring to tear him away from his sin, to give him instructions and commands to strengthen his faith and give him victory over his weakness. God is constantly concerned with the welfare of his creation. Then the Son, as if detaching himself from the triune interchange in heaven, appears on earth to redeem it; he appears as an embodiment of the divine conversation about the world, as the decision arrived at by the Father, the Son and the Spirit: namely, the salvation of mankind. Still more: the Son himself is this Word. In himself he comprises the entire substance of the divine interchange; he both is and represents it and comes to make it known to us. Something unheard-of occurs in this coming; he, the Word, dwells among us and becomes our word, and gives the strength of his being and the power of his divinity to what before was our word and our prayer. He bursts all that was in us previously. Since he is the Word, he is also prayer, and as prayer he dwells in each of us and leads us through himself, the Word, to the Father. And thus the Father gives us the key to his heaven. It is a key that never fails and that fits perfectly, because the Father himself has tested it; it was his own key to his own kingdom, and he has possessed it from all eternity. This key he has given to us, so that to some extent we can enter the eternal kingdom at any time and without a special announcement. Our prayer, therefore, is not a wild, confused clamoring and groping in the dark; it is no longer the expression of our naked creatureliness, our struggle with sin, our not knowing where to turn. Now it is the presence of the Lord. When two or three pray in his name he is among them. It is therefore the presence of eternity.

Every prayer is joined to all other prayer in the Church; for in the Lord all prayer is a praying through the one Word of the Father. Hence there is a mutual help, support and ratification of all prayers, a recognition of the presence of the Lord, who through his omniscience does not leave any praying individual alone and forsaken but rather causes him to share in the fruits of all who pray and of all prayers, even when the person praying is unaware of this and when he feels his words are weak and unworthy. His hesitation is overtaken, each time, by the fact that the Son is the Word.

From eternity one can discern two phases in which the Son leads us to the Father: the first is the conversation of man with God; the second, man's participation in the conversation of God with God. The first type of prayer can be either oral or contemplative prayer that opens man toward God, so that through God's presence he can plunge more deeply into his mysteries. He speaks and God listens. Perhaps he speaks about his own concerns that happen to occur to him: he commends to God himself, his worries, his endeavors, those dear to him, his work; or he asks God's pardon, shows him his sins or meditates on the mysteries that God reveals in Scripture; in his own words he contemplates the Word and by means of his own words he tries to understand the Word better, always in the attitude of humility and docility. Or perhaps he recites a prayer of the Church: the hours of the breviary, prayers composed by the saints, thoughts, perhaps, that he does not grasp perfectly while participating at Mass, when the deepest meaning of the individual words escapes him. But whatever form his prayer takes, if he prays with longing for truth and love, his attitude is right for God to influence and take hold of him in order to use him anywhere. By letting God's action touch him in this manner he will find his way and even lead others—acquaintances or total strangers—to God through his prayer of self-surrender.

Then there is the second phase: sharing in the conversation of the triune God, something that cannot be expressed in words and is effective beyond all imagination. It is a quietness before God, who takes the one praying into his own stillness. Perhaps as Father he gives him to the Son, or as Son he commends him to the Spirit, so that the Spirit will work in him and do in him what he wills. It is being at the disposal of the triune God, like a ball tossed from one Person to another in God. Of course there is a type of prayer that springs from a particular consecration, that of a nun, for example, who bears the name of the Holy Spirit or the Child Jesus and knows herself to be especially bound to this Person. But that should not be a limitation; rather it should serve only as a reminder of the entire divine life, and of the assent of the Mother when she conceived the Son from the Father through the Spirit. It is an assent determined by God and through which the three Persons act according to their pleasure. There is also the prayer within a special calling, the mysteries of which reveal themselves in various directions, such as a closeness to the mystery of the Spirit, or to the twelve-year-old Jesus, or to the Father as Creator of the universe;—such mysteries never manifest themselves fully in the recipient but are destined to touch others through him. These too are ever new gifts from eternal life, communicated to earth to bring it nearer to heaven, eternal grain that calls for ever-renewed sowing on earth; and when the seed springs up on earth it already belongs to eternal life. No matter which particular mystery concerns the one who prays, the total divine mystery is always implied and consequently prayer must emanate from total self-giving. Prayer may leave one waiting, show immediate effects, create openness or bring one closer to God, or do all these at once; it is a matter of indifference how God uses it, as long as it remains usable and at his disposal, as long as the one praying does not presume to calculate, to measure distances, to interpret paths or to hold on to favors in order to evaluate them.

The presence of eternal life in prayer is not only an invisible but also a visible mystery, just as prayer consists simultaneously of words and silence. When, in the Old Covenant, God spoke occasionally through the prophets, when after thirty hidden years the Son uttered his imperishable words for the space of three years, when the Spirit at Pentecost caused people to speak in strange languages, the words that reached us were very meager in comparison to the ages of the world's existence. The years of God's silence seem to be much longer. But it is not as if the word were true only when it is spoken; its truth is so rich that it reaches forward to the next utterance and back to the last one, and each points to the total truth and supplements every truth of God. But God's silence, which pertains as much to the relations of the Divine Persons as does his word, is itself filled: with his being, his immensity and eternity. To pray, therefore, means to participate not only in divine speech, but no less in divine silence, the fullness of silence that belongs to God's being. Consequently the person at prayer should consider silence—God's as well as his own—as fruitful. It does not mean emptiness, but rather fullness within being, a drawing closer that can happen without words. At prayer man can fill God's silence as well as his own with each word of God's existence, but also with his wordless being; contemplation takes him into spheres where God's existence, his action and concern for the world or simply his triune being, is sufficient. The one praying allows mystery to remain mystery in his prayer; he gazes at it and allows it to work in him, without trying to keep pace with words of explanation. He does not let himself go in carefree daydreaming; rather God can seize him, reveal his mystery to him, awaken new longings in him, make new demands on him which may simply require heightened readiness without showing the direction God's will is to take. Certainly the beginner who places himself at God's disposal needs to recognize certain guidelines in order to know that he is in the truth. As time goes on, however, God may disclose to him mysteries of the triune silence and of the eternal stillness which will remain incomprehensible to him, like an untouched treasure which God may perhaps open to him later in an unexpected manner. The person at prayer receives something that for the time being he does not need to touch, which has been handed over to him sealed up and yet belongs to him; whenever God requires it, it can be opened. It can turn into a word or become the substance of a word already received. This silence is an essential part of the God who is ever greater, who bestows eternal life on the human being as a reality into which he must grow and which his imagination can never exhaust. Even if God wished to present images of eternal life to a mystic, they would remain excerpts, adapted to those living in time and capable of any amount of intensification and expansion, since our time always limps far behind eternal time. When faith, love and hope are a living and lived reality to a Christian, he knows very well that faith constantly expands his concept of love and that love entitles him to every degree of hope. Still, this entitlement and expansion remain limited within the confines of his believing spirit. If he were willing to be expanded even more by these three virtues, somewhere he would have to stake out the outermost limits of faith and hope, knowing that in eternity God will burst them, heighten them into vision and full possession. That will be the transition into ultimate perfection. Everyone on earth recognizes that he is a sinner no matter how far he may have gone in striving for perfection, for he feels the insurmountable limits of his temporal self, limits that God will wipe away in eternity. In like manner he knows that on earth he cannot behold the Father face to face, for his capacity is insufficient until in eternity he receives full capacity from the Son who does behold the Father. It is precisely the evident difference between earthly and heavenly capacity that gives him every hope in the perfect efficacy of God when God takes him up to heaven. He knows that God holds more, much more, infinitely more in store for him. And so in word and in silence he perseveres, with the humility of one who is unworthy. Yet he is certain that God in his own good time will make him worthy, that grace can open all doors, that eternal time will eventually so take a hold of our transitory time that nothing will remain in us which could hinder us in going to God.

Each time we meditate on eternal life we gain a greater image of God. It is true that we cannot draw any conclusions about life in eternity from the course of our transitory time; but on the contrary, the strength of that which shines on us and addresses us from out of eternity may enable us to enter into a Christian relationship with our daily life, to understand the temporal better from the standpoint of eternity. While it would be idle constantly to present oneself to God as a sinner, to prove God's greatness from one's own unworthiness, it is sensible to approach God's infinity from a concept of eternity formed by prayer, Scripture and the Lord's word, and to shed light on our lives from the vantage point of God's infinity. We should not invent our own concepts of the infinite, but rather see our littleness and unworthiness in the context of infinity itself, so that in turn we may understand heaven better. Thus, we are to create new images of heaven from our old images, through the process of understanding Christian life; from meager, insufficient concepts of eternity we are to create new, fuller concepts. Eternity should play an effective part in our prayer life in order to lead us closer to God. When a person forgets himself entirely in his prayer he can feel the power of God. He is, as it were, swept away by this power; it dominates everything to such an extent that it alone remains. This presence of eternity in our prayer also strengthens and transforms our daily life and conduct—its direction is not toward eternity, but from eternity, a participation in the journey of the Son from heaven to earth. Asceticism usually shows us the way from the world to God; but much could also be gained from the opposite way. After all, at creation God sent man forth sinless into the world. Seeing our prayer and striving for perfection in this context we would be less interested in calculating our position in respect to God and instead accept as children, unconditionally, what he gives us through grace.

In his work of salvation the Son, hanging on the Cross, had each of us in mind. And the prayer that he taught us belongs to his work: as we pray we recognize our bond with him and his redemption. It is true that we can engage in all manner of considerations regarding our salvation, in order, through prayer and a life pleasing to him, to give our life some hope of eternity, out of the midst of the pain of temporal existence. But this manner of concern for our salvation, putting it foremost in our prayer, does not correspond to the Lord's attitude on the Cross. He came for all of us and died for all of us. If that has dawned on us, we too will endeavor to bear our lot in the same spirit—to pray, to act, to serve for the salvation of all, without discrimination, in him. Truly, each of us can say: the Lord died for me. And this recognition will inspire us with gratitude and a sense of profoundest obligation. But gratitude should bring us immediately to see that the Lord allows us to join our surrender, our imperfect sacrifice with his perfect one so that its effect, the striving for salvation and the approach to eternity, takes place in the spirit of the Son, that is, for all. Catholic teaching is a general teaching, given by the Lord for all. Hence every member of the Church must let the Lord govern his prayer and his life to such an extent that it will be used for those purposes which he alone can discern and which finally flow into the salvation of all. As a person under obedience prefers not to determine his own course, but lets himself be guided by obedience, likewise, when we pray "Thy will be done on earth as it is in heaven", we should refrain from trying to determine which fruit of salvation our prayer shall produce or which aspect of the general redemption is being promoted by it.

7

The Gate of Vision

For the unbeliever, faith in the eternal things can only be a construct of the imagination, combined with a secret dishonesty which draws a veil over man's existence as it really is. He cannot come to terms with his existence, with his expectations of life and finally with his disappearance from it and therefore escapes into a fictitious world whose deceptive contents can never be proved by his sober reason. It is different with the man of faith. He knows that through faith he has access to God's world, a world without shadow and impurity, where there is room only for the wholly divine and eternal. His faith is empowered to open spheres for him that are not accessible to reason or to human calculation. He turns from himself and simply believes in God, leaves even his faith to God, so that it may be capable of any expansion and new fulfillment. For him the firmest reality is the word of God, which opens up for him the hidden kingdom of truth and leads him into it. He has built up his life on this word; he hopes that this word may fulfill his life. This hopeful and effective faith is prayer. Like all who live in time, he too is often tired, fainthearted and downcast; frequently shame holds him back from throwing himself through prayer into the bosom of God. He lets the flight of his faith be impeded by worries, calculations and longings. Then for a time his view into the hidden reality is veiled. This experience frightens him and causes him to renew the trust that leaves everything to God. The more his prayer carries him away from himself, so much more does God's world open up to him. His eyes open: he sees. He can see quite simply what he utters in his prayer: the prayer of the Church, the prayer of the Lord in Scripture. He contemplates what they say: he gazes at God whom he adores, at the saints whom he venerates, at heaven for which he hopes. He sees them with the eyes of faith. These eyes of faith open to the degree in which he submits himself to the object of his faith's adoration: he wishes to serve, to be at God's disposal, to fulfill the demands made on him by the divine world. To begin with he is given a number of earthly concepts and images from Scripture, words that the Lord spoke for him, the entire system of Christian doctrine that applies to him as to everyone else. But the reality underlying all this becomes real only to faith engaged in prayer. Through the presence of the Spirit in every prayer this reality takes on life and form, grows personal, and is transformed into something he can understand, something which fulfills his longing, something into which his existence fits as if it were predetermined, something to which he gladly submits. He does not wish to miss anything that God offers: not from egotism that desires the most for itself, but from a sense of simple Christian service which recognizes that everything God shows is intended for the whole Church.

God can go further and permit his servant to see excerpts from his heavenly world, no longer simply in obedient meditation on the revealed word as the Holy Spirit interprets it in the heart, but rather in seeing and hearing things that are shown to him directly and uniquely from heaven. This experience, too, occurs in a spirit of catholicity. Sometimes these are things that have nothing to do with the subject of his present prayer or meditation but are nevertheless an answer to his attitude. For instance, he may be suddenly interrupted in the veneration of a saint by some truth of the Spirit, formerly remote to him, which at first glance he cannot even grasp. But it is genuine vision and a fragment of heaven and he must incorporate it into what he already knows about heaven from the Church, from Scripture and from preaching. There is no preparation for this kind of vision; it occurs each time like lightning, and takes possession of the person in a manner foreshadowing what it will be like to be taken possession of by eternal life.

Some mystics have seen whole heavenly chronicles, apparently without any gaps. For instance they followed the course of the Lord's life and Passion on earth as it was viewed from heaven. Others experienced more abstract truths; still others received jumbled images that seemed to follow no order or have no inner connection with each other. But all that is inessential. The important thing is that every genuine vision is heaven approaching earth and a filling of human faith through eternal life. This is because all faith is nourished by heaven and has its substance in the triune God, who is shown forth by the Son, announced by the prophets and given in the Church, from which every believer receives whatever God has planned for him and his vocation requires. The unsystematic visions are in a sense erratic and thus appear to the rational mind to be unreliable, for reason cannot perceive the usefulness of such isolated insights; reason seeks knowledge in the integration of cumulative regularities. But in visions God can waive every law of cognition; he can reveal something completely remote which yet is connected with what is close at hand, without revealing some or even any of the connecting links. One can perhaps claim that in visions sovereignty and absolute freedom belong to God, whereas regularity belongs to the Church. But rules must be subject to this will of God. And understanding must come into action where God's lightning has struck. No new truth can come to light without having a connection with what has gone before; it is the duty of the Church to discover the connections and links and to integrate the new gift into her treasury of truth. Perhaps the visionary can contribute to this process by contemplating in his experience not only the word in its immediate context but also the threads that tie it to truths already known, without thereby losing sight of the suddenness, uniqueness and amazing quality of his vision. Generally speaking, every vision of heavenly things contains something of the "beyond" that eludes all attempts at adaptation and classification. Anyone hearing an account of such an experience might think he had understood it exactly and entirely; at most he will have grasped only an important part, albeit perhaps the most important part. This "beyond" does not mean that what has been expressed is only relatively accurate, leaving the shimmering background of heavenly, eternal life blurred and confused. It does mean, however, that an attitude of total openness is indispensable for correct comprehension, both for the mystic and for the person who interprets and guides the experience. After Ignatius had seen some shining thing at Manresa he could not explain it for a long time; much later he understood that it was a delusion of the devil. At first he was influenced by the vision in a manner incomprehensible to himself, while he remained at prayer and clung to his faith. His inability to integrate the phenomenon was neither spiritual nor moral imperfection. The only thing required of him was to remain in obedience; the explanation occurred at a moment ordained by God. Generally speaking, even the strangest experience has some sort of comprehensibility, since at least part of it is intended to be translated and has an immediately relevant meaning—either for the visionary himself or for others who are meant to experience something through him.

Genuine prayer transforms a human being. The person who prays bears within himself a substance that changes him. First and foremost, this substance is the Lord whom he receives in Communion and the purity of grace given him in absolution; but it is also his abiding within the sphere of eternal life, that is, the attitude of prayer. It opens him so that God can take charge of him and make him better able to obey his voice. It draws him away from his atmosphere of sin and transports him into a heavenly environment, without alienating him from the world or causing him to lose his way in it. The praying person can lead the active life required of him; he can and should be wholly involved in it, aware of everything around him, using to the full his faculties of perception and judgment. Even if he leads a life of pure contemplation, he may not be deaf to the world with its miseries and demands, for the reason behind his choice of vocation was the invitation to work together with the Son for the redemption of the world here below. And redemption of the world requires a certain insight into the nature of the world. When the Lord bore our sins on the Cross they did not lie in a clotted mass of filth and misery upon him; rather, with clear perception he could have called each one by name. Therefore no follower of Jesus may turn his back on the world, no matter how close the Lord may draw him to himself; for the world is the Father's creation, and it and no other is the object of the Son's redemption. But prayer enables man to understand God's eternal purposes with the world, and in order to reach this understanding he must first learn to understand God's own nature, the relationship of the Divine Persons and their eternal conversation about everything that concerns the world and determines its fate. Hence he cannot regard eternal life either as an abstraction or as an isolated entity, but rather in its connection with earth, as the will of the Father to redeem the world through the Son, the most real connection possible between God and man. Furthermore, once he has entered heaven, he will not be able to dwell there without continually looking back at earth, as long as it remains. Even in eternal life he will be bound to stay in a close relationship to the world. As long as one sinner remains on earth the door between heaven and earth will not be closed. No seclusion from the world will be possible. Certainly the direct vision of God will plunge everything into a new light, into a new and essential relationship of dependence, but the world will not disappear in God. For the Son does not cease to redeem the world. And he will never withhold from those who are his own the vision of his work and of their cooperation. Hence one can say that no one who experienced on earth the blissful presence of the Lord in prayer would have been capable of this experience without at the same time being firmly rooted in the world. He experiences heaven from the standpoint of earth in a relationship of solidarity, in submission to the details of

God's will, which is manifest—among other ways —in this bliss experienced by the one praying, who is surrounded by sinners and himself belongs to their ranks. This bliss is a sign from heaven experienced by a human being who also experiences the signs of the world. The vision occurs at an axis of exchange and relationship. The great Saint Teresa did not stop cooking her fish during an ecstasy, nor in heaven does she stop admonishing her daughters on earth.

8

The Eternal Life of the Father and Creation

The Father created the world not just out of nothing, but also out of his thought. All things that come to be are an expression of his presence, his will and his being. Certainly creation is the origin of our passing time and not the beginning of God's time, which is eternal. Still, our time was carved out of eternity, set in contrast to it, characterized and determined by it. Passing time was created with a view to the time which does not pass away; for the present the two run parallel, but the former will be taken up into the latter in the end. The Father separates day and night, man can begin to count; but he learns to count from the number of days of the Father's creation. Man acquaints himself with the things created during those days by counting them, but also by gazing at the Creator who looks on his work and deems it good. All things have a twofold relationship to the Creator: they are made on a particular day, and they are judged to be good. Their derivation from God is ratified by the movement back to him expressed in this judgment of his. God creates them out of himself, but he receives them back in finding them good. And if that is true of all things and of all living beings and of man, it applies also to time and to everything that occurs and will occur in the course of it. Day and night are independent of man; they have always been there, the unchanging framework of his fleeting history, of his achievements and his judgments. They are part of the original stability of God's creation which expresses his will and his being, the creation which at the end of time will flow into God's eternity—not to disappear, but to make eternal in God everything that happened during the temporal days and nights, according to God's design. Thus time has always borne a relationship to eternity. When the Creator walks in Paradise he does not separate himself from his eternity; he gives man a sense of the presence and the atmosphere of eternity in a way he can understand. He gives man senses that can perceive his voice and his walking through the garden. When sin dulls this faculty of sensing God's presence, even extinguishing it to the point that man is capable of denying God, the eternal permanence is not affected. God lives on within it; the sinner cannot drive him out of his time. God's time belongs to himself. He will invite whomever he considers worthy to share his time with him, those created for this sharing who have spent their lives with that goal in mind. God gives his creature the grace necessary to reach his goal. He shows him the paths he must take. He does not allow his straying into perishableness to become definitive and final, but plans means to overcome this turning-away. In Paradise the distance between God and man could not be measured: God came and went; he spoke in a perceptible manner designed to inspire man with obedience without burdening him with a problematical distinction between God and himself. But when sin occurred the abyss yawned between them; man hid from himself and from God and tried to cover himself with leaves. But God did not accept this flight; he sought man out in his hiding place. This has been the story of God and man ever since: every new attempt of man to conceal himself from God has been overtaken again and again when God finds him.

Later the presence of God was revealed to the prophets in various ways. They too were overwhelmed repeatedly in their faith by the supernatural, miraculous being of God. They were not permitted in any way to settle down in their faith on earth in order to fulfill the task assigned to them by faith or reason. They were not allowed to reckon their time as if it belonged to them. Even the days at their disposal had a way of eluding their grasp, because God's constantly renewed interventions in time were required for them and for their people. The how and why of these interventions remained a total mystery of God and his eternity. No prophet was able of himself to say, "On such or such a day God will speak or act." And if he ever could say it, it was only because God had revealed it to him. Of himself it was impossible to speak thus; there was no step from our calculable time into God's uncalculated and incalculable time. So great was the triumph, the superior power of heaven. One can discern features of God's eternal being from this triumph, and from man's defeat. God placed the prophet, however, in a sort of middle zone between his triumph and man's defeat and gave him insight that enabled him to survey the things of earth to a certain extent, but also to view more closely the mysteries of heaven.

God created man not to intimidate him but to love him. Before the first sin the relationship between God and man was one of harmony. From all eternity God loved the being he intended to create. And man, standing before his Creator and hearing his voice, loved him according to his own powers. Neither needed to define the other any more closely in order to maintain their relationship. God had destined man to be king over all created things, had ordained his growth and increase, and had given him his love, destined for him from all eternity, to accompany him along his path. Man therefore found the world already created for his purposes. He did not need to make further dispositions because everything was good and in its designated place. All he was required to do was simply to accept God's judgment of the goodness of creation in an act of obedience that would not have cost him any self-conquest, because God stood in full clarity above him and God's pure judgment was perfectly valid for him. But when he found himself alienated from God through sin, he had to begin defining God. That is, in everything he undertook, good as well as evil, he had to try to recapture God's judgment, envision God's actions on the basis of his own, decide whether God's attitude was approval or rejection, permission or prohibition. Through sin man shifted not only himself but all creation from the right relationship with God. A sign of the disturbed order was that God no longer spoke to man directly, but henceforth through mediators appointed to the task. In the state of alienation in which man found himself, he was better able to understand these voices. From now on angels are sent on missions to mankind. Angels stand directly before God in eternity. They convey what they receive of his eternal wisdom, which to them in heaven is self-evident, and they must make it palatable to man on earth. Each message is a breakthrough into perishable time, bringing eternity close. Certain of these breakthroughs brought something permanently valid into time, as for example the law of Moses; certain others, particular prophecies, were given for a definite situation; they were valid as coming from God, but also in a certain sense transitory, because they were issued for a given time. They too were intended to bring eternity closer, to enlarge the image of God, to proclaim his power over time, to show his omniscience and providence as definitive for man. Then came other prophecies revealing that God is not alone in his heaven but enjoys a unique inner vitality, filling heaven as space and eternity as time, its intimacy, however, withheld from man's knowledge. That was more than Adam was permitted to see. Adam saw God as one individual, entering into a relationship with himself. But in the Old Covenant there were indications of a mysterious inner life in God, hints that God in his mystery possessed sovereign power in full concentration and imparted some of it to his servants and mediators. The existence of angels gave man an inkling that in heaven the various tasks are apportioned, that there is a multiplicity in eternal life, a whole society that not only lives in God, but also is commissioned by God to cooperate in man's return to God. In doing so the angels make men's alienation and perishableness more endurable, showing them in various ways that they are not abandoned, but rather that God is forging new links with them. And when men began to despair over their fate and felt their existence to be useless and degraded, God showed them in the prophetic promises that he did not despair of the goodness of creation, that there was still a relationship with him and that through the consent of a human being he would open the way for his Son's Incarnation. Immense rays of hope illuminated the vast power of God and of eternity over man and his time, but the care of the Creator for his world was also revealed—all of which could be interpreted only as love. And all God's words of condemnation, the darkness surrounding him, his silences, his sending his people into exile were all measures to be overcome in the approaching new era instituted by God. God himself used them to set limits, announce conclusions and also to indicate new beginnings, the descent of the Son and his birth of the Virgin.

Seen from the vantage point of the Old Covenant, these are all promises of the Father. The cooperation of the Son and the Spirit remains veiled. The purpose of this veil is above all to shed light on the omnipotence of the Father, his sovereignty in his decisions and also his continuing responsibility for the world which he had created. The New Covenant will provide a complementary point of view; it shows the will of the Son, in harmony with the will of the Father. It shows his decision from all eternity to put himself at the disposal of the world's redemption and to send forth the Spirit to seal his work. Since no one on earth has ever seen the Father, whereas the Son was revealed in human form and the Spirit in various visible signs, the Old Testament is the clearest exposition of the Father. The promises of the prophets, the voice which they heard, the tables of the law, written by God's own finger, the burning bush, the whispering wind on Mount Horeb—all of these are acts of the Father, in which the cooperation of the Son and the Spirit can only be surmised. From the standpoint of the Old Covenant it is the Father who promises, the Father who sends, the Father who exposes the world again and again to the workings of his fatherly eternity.

Seen from eternity, time appears as nothing, for the Father did not take a piece out of eternity, which is in God's possession, in order to furnish it for the world. Such "eternal time" would not be useful or proper for the creatures of the Father. On the other hand, he could not let the special time which he invented for them simply disappear into nothingness; rather he placed it face to face with his eternity, letting it become itself through this proximity. A deep analogy exists between the two. When on earth Easter is celebrated there is a corresponding eternal joy—not in the sense that heaven conforms to earth, but in such a way that divine eternity is open and inclined toward human time. When the Church arrives on the scene with her new feasts the relations between time and eternity change once again, because the feasts are marked not only by the Father but also by the Son who was man and by the Spirit who dwells within these feasts and perfects them. In the Old Covenant the Father impresses his own image; in the New it is impressed by the Son who is consubstantial with the Father and who speaks to men in human language. So the mysteries dwelling in the intimacy of God, whose existence and secrecy are hinted at in the Old Testament, are now unsealed to the world. A part of this intimacy is the image that the Son has of the Father. We can see what the Father is like by looking at the Son, his word and his being. Even among human beings there is a great difference between simply introducing oneself and being described by a friend. The Son possesses this power of giving testimony in its fullness, for he knows from eternal experience what he speaks about in time. He takes upon himself the task of revealing the Father within the Father's creation. And when the Spirit comes and the disciples begin to speak in tongues, it is not simply a continuation of the Old Testament prophecy, but a new revelation of the Father, now taken up by the third Divine Person. Now that the Spirit dwells in human hearts the heavenly words are both near and clear to mankind. No longer are they a foreign language, but the Christian's "Father tongue". There were isolated miracles in the Old Testament, coming down from heaven to give testimony to God's power; but with the coming of the Son the power of miracles is transferred into the will of a man who, because he is God, can choose the time and occasion to work the miracle. So the Father's entire miraculous world has broken into earthly time.

9

The Eternal Life of the Son and Redemption

The appearance of the Son instills immense hope in the hearts of the faithful. They experience that the promises are fulfilled in him, and the fulfillment is greater than the promise, since the Son, while basing himself on the promises, yet bestows more (because he is God) and does so immediately. Christians share in this overwhelming meeting of the Father's heaven with the sinners' earth, accomplished in the Son, perfectly joining eternal and transitory time. First of all, a great change has occurred in respect to the Father: he no longer needs to proclaim himself as "the Lord your God, who punishes and shows mercy from generation to generation", who lets his eternity be measured according to the passing human generations. Now the Son can bear witness to him, the Son who loves him and knows him, who lives with him from all eternity. The Father's world, which was separate—he did walk in Paradise, but not directly in the sinners' world—now becomes an accessible world whose gates stand wide open. The Son, who is God and represents the Father, lives among us, shares our days and nights, submits to the laws made by the Father governing our world. There is no longer an inaccessible "there" and the familiar "here" which everywhere encounters the limits of mortality, but a genuine compatibility of both in the Son. The Father is seen by mankind, represented by the Son. The truth of the Old Testament bursts open in the Incarnation into an undreamed-of love. The Son lives like one of us; his fellow man can observe him and reflect on his words and deeds. The goodness and divinity of these words and deeds awaken in the human heart an immediate echo: the heart understands this language and feels understood in it. A human basis is formed—a solid, sound basis of fellowship and trust. Anyone who approaches the Son as the gate will reach the Father, for the Son's being on earth leads to the being in heaven, and his teaching in human words belongs in heaven to the Father; it is part of the exchange among the three Divine Persons in eternity. The Son brings the entire eternal life to earth, not keeping it a secret from the other life, but desiring to bestow it directly. No one crosses his path without receiving something of it. The Son is born, grows up, works, lives day to day as any other human being. But he stamps everything with a divine value through his perfect obedience and shares this divine value with his brethren by giving himself to them. The Eucharist is nothing other than a sharing in his Divine Being; everyday things—bread and wine—become bearers of his immortalized Body and Blood and bestow on those who receive them the presence of divine life. The disciples who take part in the journeying, working and preaching of the Son know that they are sharing in a revelation of heaven: "You have the words of eternal life!" The Son did not separate himself from the Father through the Incarnation. He lives in his intimacy. The Son lives and communicates the divine reality so directly that his fellow humans can form an idea of the boundlessness of eternal life. They are to partake of it even now, in a way not incompatible with their narrow human life. When the Father walked in Paradise, the two kinds of time were side by side: God in his eternity was there and man in his temporalness was also there. The Son, however, lives among us and even within us. He stands with his eternity in the midst of our time. Initially he seemed to occupy time and space like any other human being: first he stood on this spot, then someone else stood there; the cup he once used is now used by someone else. But after the

Resurrection his space comes closer to us and even enters into us, so that his space and ours coincide. We live, yet not we, but he lives in us. A bit of our daily life is taken into his eternal life. In the beginning the Father judged his creatures good; they had this quality insofar as they were a part of creation in the world. But when the Father repeats his judgment now, this goodness which he recognizes in things has come from his eternity and is applicable to it; through the Son all things have matured for eternal life. And the Son's endeavors are directed toward infusing them with ever more eternal goodness.

As a result of this, evil too is changed in character. It is what is separated, alien, turned away from eternity. But the Son wishes to touch it in order to turn it in his direction. In the New Covenant conversion, the turning toward the Father through the Son, is present in a much more extensive sense than in the Old. Any individual can be touched at any time by the Son, who never ceases to send forth his Spirit to encounter each person, who never ceases to be the eternal Word of the Father offering himself to every sinner to compel him to conversion. Evil is seen in its true colors on the Cross, where the Lord bears all sins. On the Cross it was vanquished—not just once, but continuously: because the absolution instituted by the Son to demonstrate the triumphant power of the Cross can be imparted anew every day, because the sinner can always find access to the Lord through the Church, and to the Father through the Lord. In this process evil has lost some of its sinister character, because it can be expressed in speech in order to be wiped out. On the other hand, it has acquired a personal gravity which can be measured in the generosity of the Crucified as he offers himself to endure the blow of each individual sin. Each sinner can ascertain what a terrible effect his sin has caused. But the life of the Son has set limits to the power of evil over the things of this world. Up to the moment of confession they are bad; after confession on the way to the Father they are good, for they are under the blessing of the Son. The world which man has created is shrinking; but the world into which the Father invites the brothers of his Son for all eternity is expanding and growing more definitive and more infinite. The Son bears this world within him, and it is simultaneously the world of the Father and of the Spirit.

From now on we can see our neighbor as someone destined for eternal life. For the unbeliever, life in common with us is subject to the laws of nature and humanity; but for us, something more profound governs this life together, namely the destiny of eternal life for which this life is a preparation. The believer knows and worships the triune God and recognizes in prayer a foreshadowing of eternal life. His words, which God hears, reach their destination in God: he receives them, gives them an ultimate meaning in eternity and relates the praying person to this meaning. In this manner the concepts of our daily life are immeasurably expanded. The Son is an example of this. Apparently his Incarnation is a narrowing of his eternity, his carrying the Cross a terrible burden on his divine freedom. But it took place to effect a corresponding expansion of life in each individual. The more the Son becomes a mere human being, so much more does he open the gate of infinity for man. His increasing accommodation to our finiteness stands in inverse proportion to our increasing participation in his eternal life.

That is why there can be no question of a blurring of eternity and time. Acting on earth in the name of the Father and the Spirit, of the whole triune life, the Son constantly knows and experiences in his vision that God is in heaven and is living his eternal life there, while he, the Son, lives his daily life on earth. It would be a mistake to see in the eternal life mediated by the Son only an expansion of earthly life, a repetition on a grander scale of what we experience here below, or to think that every right concept which contains a piece of truth in this world would only need to be developed a little further in order to possess eternal validity. In spite of the self-surrender of the Son the divine mysteries remain beyond our ken; they are kept in store by the Church, who does not herself know what they are, who is unable to count her treasures. Every word of the Son is more momentous than we can imagine; it is open to the speech of the triune God, so devoted to him that it can accomplish everything God has planned from all eternity. If we took our understanding of Christian doctrine and tried to divide it into sections, we would realize that each section is prolonged invisibly into heaven, into an expansion over which God disposes at his pleasure. But it would be wrong to gather the sections together in such a way that there would be no space between them on earth for whatever God is still planning, still possesses and still is. As one day in heaven can hardly be confused with one day on earth, so the Son's divinity and his humanity cannot be equated. He did not reduce his divinity to fit it into the format of our humanity; rather he took on human form—something completely new—to be like us and to let us take part in the totally new life of the Father. If no human science will ever reach a state in which it is able to predict future discoveries and advances, if the finest human system must allow for the unexpected, it is all the more true of the future experience of God and of eternal life. For it will not be man who, by adding together all temporal experiences of the divine, will be able to construct the vision of God; it will be God who, according to his measure and his discretion, will give us the experience of himself, the possession of his eternal life and the full view of his infinity.

When the Son returns to heaven the disciples see him disappear in the cloud; it is like a natural phenomenon. But they understand what is meant thereby, namely the heaven of eternity, the return to the Father and divine, eternal life. They remain on earth and all that they know will remain piecemeal. But they have recognized one thing: the attitude of heaven toward earth, the generosity of the Father who gave his Son out of love for the world. And the new hope which is granted them is now the basis for everything. It gives to faith and love that final form that makes them worth living for in the Christian sense. In the future, no act of faith or love can be self-sufficient but can be opened completely toward God through hope. And this is true of every work, every deed accomplished in the Christian life: they belong to the eternal vision, are taken up into it and prepare the way toward it. The unity of action and contemplation has received its final meaning in the Son's return to heaven. All that man does on earth is action performed for God so that man may share in the eternal contemplation. His earthly life is preparation for his eternal life; his doing is preparation for his eternal being. Even if the earthly work of a believer consists in a contemplative life where his prayer and his existence are entirely at the disposal of the Son, this earthly contemplation remains a preparation for the true and definitive contemplation in heaven; for his life as a religious is basically not very different from that of the active orders, insofar as he forms a community with all the praying persons on earth. This earthly community can be termed active in comparison to the eternal contemplation to which the Father invites everyone through his incarnate Son with the Holy Spirit.

10

The Eternal Life of the Spirit and Consummation

Divine revelation is progressive: in the Old Covenant the Father revealed himself with reticence; the incarnate Son brought a closeness and clarity, and finally the Spirit places the work of Father and Son in the clearest light and at Pentecost gives himself personally. From the first moment of his coming he appears as one who is sent. In the case of the incarnate Son, who came to fulfill the prophecies of the Father, this attribute of having been sent manifested itself only gradually. In the descent of the Spirit it is primary. He is sent by the Son but at the same time by the Father; being sent by the Son would make no sense without his being sent also by the Father. In coming, the Spirit confirms the Son. First of all he confirms the mission of the Son, who fulfilled the promises of the Old Covenant; and secondly he confirms the return of the Son to heaven, since the Son promised to send the Spirit from heaven. By making this promise the Son showed that heaven would remain open to earth even after his Ascension. Heaven would not cease in its care for earth. Just as God did not abandon Adam in the world, so the Son did not forsake his Apostles. Heaven remains open. There are still promises to be fulfilled.

But the Spirit does not only confirm; he also creates new things according to his nature. By breathing where he wills he gives evidence of his divinity, strengthening and vivifying what the Son left behind; he continually invents new forms and vessels for the body of teaching within the Church founded by the Son. In his breathing he chooses apostles, newly called to the faith, and endows them with the power of hearing and responding. He gives the power of a new spirit of faith to enliven doctrine, to discover concealed truths in it and to make them accessible to human beings. The Spirit is God and as God does not separate himself from the Father or the Son. He brings them with him, as earlier he was the bearer of the Father's seed when the Son became man. He is the bearer of doctrine, bearer of the living substance that is constantly descending to instill new life, life from the triune God, life which is released in order to draw man into God. Coming from the Father and the Son, the Spirit goes to man to bestow on him the fruits of his origin. He returns laden with that which men have discovered, explained, bestowed and received by his power for the enrichment of the Church. The Christian spirit's gifts to the Church never flow directly from the individual minister to the Church, but take part in the way of the Holy Spirit; they are borne to heaven by the Spirit, thence to fall on the Church like rain and be received in the vessels waiting for them.

On the morning of Pentecost the Spirit comes in the form of fiery tongues which are present without intermediary and bring forth newness equally without intermediary. Even when the Spirit ratifies anything, he does so in a creative manner; indeed, in his creating is the ratification. He transforms. He converts. He lets light appear, shows things in bold outline, reveals thoughts that are all related in that they are divine thoughts imparted to man. To produce life and to give testimony [*Zeugen und Bezeugen*] are one and the same to the Spirit. In giving testimony he gives life to himself, in testifying to both the Father and the Son. His testimony is a continual effervescence, giving birth to new testimony, summoning and bestowing it, for man of himself would be incapable of finding the word of testimony except through the Spirit. When those who are moved by the Spirit speak in tongues, they are suddenly empowered to hear and utter words that are not their own, either in terms of sound and structure, or in terms of content. Each of their human words gives testimony to the Word given by God. The explosive expansion is to be found in the Word itself. And the human spirit itself is burst open by the Divine Spirit and newly consecrated. And since no one can speak in tongues or be converted except under strictest obedience to the triune God, this obedience is both required and bestowed by the Spirit. The Spirit is always the answer to the question that he poses.

Wherever the Spirit blows, he is always presenting an image of eternal life. Each time perhaps only a small image, but it is a projection of the heavenly image, an excerpt from the whole; and when sometimes this fragment does not seem to fit the contours and shadings of the whole, seeming now shrivelled up, now a rank growth, it will eventually prove that it belongs. Perhaps, too, the Spirit gives man a kind of eyeglasses to perceive the image in the manner intended by the Spirit, so that it will then combine with other images to form in the Spirit a perfect whole. The heaven of the Spirit is in motion, for the Spirit is the exchange of love between the Father and the Son. It was not difficult to love the incarnate God. It is made even easier for those who come after the first disciples to discover in the humanity of the Son his heavenly being. But it can become extremely difficult for man when he is asked, on the basis of the Spirit's blowing where he wills, not only to form a conception of the Spirit's eternal life but also to love him and the eternity which he mediates. It is the same with the sacraments. The grace received at baptism, matrimony, ordination, confession and Communion has a distinct character in each case. This is not so clear at confirmation. Certainly it makes man a mature Christian in the community, a defender of the faith in the world. That is why he receives the Spirit. But it is difficult for the Christian to distinguish the Spirit in his experience of faith from his own faith, his own understanding, from what he calls his own spirit. The Spirit, however, is nevertheless the great Other who gives himself in ever-renewed, difficult encounters between the divine and the human spirit. Man must bear the Spirit within himself, in order to arrive at an image of eternity—less for himself than for others—that is attractive and inviting. The Christian takes on the duties of the apostolate and thus the insight into his own mission, not to bask in it or to determine his destiny through psychological speculations or to arrive at deeper self-knowledge, but rather to understand in clearer outline and to accept the factual content of his mission which is being communicated to him anew by the Spirit, and the demands it makes upon him. But that means losing oneself to make

God's dwelling in man more habitable, to give the Son a free hand and to let the Father see the implementing of his will in man. In this respect the Spirit is like someone who gets a house ready for habitation, while man only makes the space available and lets the Spirit in. To let him in means, however, that from now on man will never be without him or be finished with him, since the divine will, for which the Spirit prepares a dwelling, will take over the entire space. This expropriation is freely given through faith, but it grows increasingly thorough and fundamental because God's will is that which is always greater. In this we have a presentiment of what being in the Spirit will mean in eternal life.

This expropriation creates a certain objectivity. Man is to feel chosen and let his subjectivity be determined on that basis. He should consider that God has precise plans for him and matter-of-factly submit himself to them. Both the acceptance of the objective mission and its achievement in his own life are the work of the Holy Spirit. Both enable man to grow more aware of God's objective purposes and thereby to ready himself for an eternal life which is not merely suited to his own wishes, longings and personal hopes, but corresponds to God's being in eternity. The Spirit working on man does not rob him of his personality or reduce him to a nameless and lifeless tool, which could comply more fully with the demands upon it only by self-annihilation. On the contrary, it releases the personality planned by God so that it opens uniquely to the Spirit in order to attain its eternal destiny. This personality fulfills itself in the divine will and will stand before God for all eternity in an adoration reserved for it alone and imparted to it by the Spirit. Here eternal life finally loses the restricted character commonly attributed to it by human imagination. It is full of such objective bliss that only the objectivity of the Divine Spirit can transmit it. When God forbade the Jews to carve an image of him, it was for the sake of a greater freedom, namely the freedom to receive from God his own image and not be satisfied with the offspring of their imagination. They themselves were to become images of God and act as his living, spiritual canvases so that God's brush could retouch and alter them as he pleased. Not until he sent his Son did God give the definitive image of himself. This image returns to heaven and sends a new one: the living flame of Pentecost morning that was to burn the heavenly image into the hearts of the faithful. These flames have such a purifying effect that in the future each true image of God can come directly from him, for now souls are capable of receiving his image in humility. They are no longer dependent on their own images but look to the Son in order to be transformed, here on earth, through the Spirit, into the image of divine eternity.

11

The Presence of Eternal Life

The Father did not create the world in opposition to heaven but in relation to it. Earth belongs to heaven. And mankind is created for heaven. The heaven of the triune God, with every infinity at its disposal, has enough space to accommodate earth and its inhabitants in the manner decreed by the Father. To the people in the Old Covenant dreams and visions and the voices heard by the prophets all presented small excerpts from a heaven of constant motion and vitality, exhibiting the most varied theophanies. Through the coming of the Son the way from earth to heaven became a quite different one. The word spoken on the Cross, "Today you will be with me in paradise", shows that the distance between transitory and eternal life can be crossed in the space of a "today". The Son has shortened the distance, not only in his words spoken on earth, but also in the vision which he confers on those who are his own. "You will see the heavens open", he promises his disciples. Stephen gazes into this opened heaven and sees the Son of Man sitting at the right hand of God. He dies in the Lord, who immediately becomes, for him, the gate. Many persons have seen the heavens open either at the moment of their death or on other occasions, and have taken part in the celebrations of heaven and seen the activity of the Blessed Trinity in such a way as to glean a valid and lasting impression, however inadequate, of eternal life. If one were to collate all that Christians have seen of heaven, certain recurrent aspects would predominate: for instance, the way the Son likes to show images of the glorification of his Mother, designed to give his followers on earth an idea of eternal life. Still, the visions never duplicate one another; they evince related characteristics, but never the same ones, because eternity is not monotony but fullness of life. When the Father created man in his image and likeness he gave him some of his own sense of the ever-newness of existence, of life and of the Spirit. If one imagines God only as simple, unified and at rest, as philosophers often do, it would seem that the main problem of creation was solved for God through the Incarnation of the Son, namely the return of earth's spatial and temporal diversity to the unity of heaven. And once that had been achieved, the tension in which the Father watched and accompanied his Son on earth would be released, slackened and extinguished. God would be relieved of the problematical earth and could return to the peace and quiet of eternity. What an impoverishment of the concept of eternal life and God's care for creatures! If it were true, one would expect that, in order to break the boredom of his eternity, God would be always looking around for new involvements, new worlds to create in an effort to provide stimulation. But God is love, and his eternal life is one of love; it has no need for another life to fill eternity with that stimulation. When we have once awakened to love and begun to live out of love, that is, out of God and his eternity, we will understand what infinite riches are hidden in it and how it alone can be forever new for all eternity—new for God and new for man, in an inexhaustible fruitfulness. As his earthly life unfolds, the average man discovers in it a growing simplification: with increasing age his intensity, his interest decreases; he becomes more distanced, he feels as if he has been clarified. If, however, he remains alive in his faith through the action of the Holy Spirit, he experiences no diminishing in faith in spite of the slackening powers of his spirit. Perhaps he knows even less than before how his own spirit relates to the Holy Spirit, yet he knows himself infallibly to be a partaker, through the Spirit, in a plenitude of ever-new truth (which his natural faculties may not be able to discern, though it belongs to him as a believer). Only in eternal life will he be able to encounter this pressing fullness with his own spirit; but that does not prevent him from living in it already by right. The dissociation between his failing powers and the sustained power and vitality of the mysteries of faith will thus lead him to an experience of what is waiting for him in eternal life. Heaven is not something simple, defined once and for all. It is the kingdom of God. And if on earth we already have received a certain presentiment of the inexhaustibility of divine life, we can be certain that it belongs completely to heaven.

We experience the same thing in the prayer of adoration. In the Church we speak of "perpetual adoration". But we know how quickly we tire of it. Even if our spirit is eager and longs for more, we must still leave off because the body cannot keep up; it grows weak and needs sleep and refreshment. And thus we see again the disparity between the need for a continuance proper to adoration—even the limited kind of which our spirit is capable—and the demands of perishable life. Here we have the beginning of the experience of what will be perpetual adoration in heaven. How we would like to jump over the barriers of our bodies! Eventually they will fall when we shall be creatures of eternity, seized by a tireless ability to pray, because we shall behold an inexhaustible wealth of new things in the vision of God which will simply compel our adoration. Then, remaining at prayer will be part of blessedness. We will not have to count the hours any more, fearful of having to stop; every stroke of the hour will be submerged in timelessness.

Faith tells us that we are destined to be vessels of the Holy Spirit; we know by name the qualities and the gifts which the Spirit brings us. Since the Lord sends the Spirit to us we cannot say that man is simply not adapted to receive him. And yet every believer knows how insufficiently he places himself at the Spirit's disposal and how many obstacles he puts in his way. From the example of others, for example the saints, he can see that there are better ways of doing it, much better. The seven gifts of the Holy Spirit are perhaps only abstract words for him, for his dullness prevents him from appreciating their perfect vitality. He has to describe the Spirit in human terms in order to understand him, and yet knows that this anthropomorphism is inadmissible. Hence his own incapacity leads him to envisage eternal life as a place where the Spirit can work freely; where all who receive him are completely open to his breathing and are perfectly holy; where the pallid concepts of the Spirit's characteristics are filled out and experienced.

And faith remains veiled. Both in recognizing and in giving witness to the Spirit in the world the believer feels constricted. He struggles for greater insight and strength, but he does not achieve them. In striving toward God—even if he has the faith of a saint—he remains attached to human concepts. And even with the concept of heroic virtue, he does not become free before God in the final plenitude of freedom. But God gives to such struggling faith a foretaste of this fullness of freedom and a great longing to press forward with every power to attain it. This struggling and pressing forward is always the effect of the Holy Spirit. The Spirit is best empowered to make himself understood. The essence of heroic virtue is to exceed the human average; but there can be no determination of an average, since from the start the demands made on the Christian's natural powers are superhuman. This overtaxing keeps him constantly in suspense and often makes his Christian destiny difficult to comprehend. It is a prelude to the bursting forth of eternal life that will no longer be overtaxing of our strength, but the superabundant fulfillment of God's expectations for us, of that in his question which brought the word "overtaxing" to our lips here on earth. And if in eternity, by the power of the Spirit, we no longer live in a state of overtaxation, it will be because while on earth the Lord met these superhuman demands—accepted by the Father and the Spirit as well as himself—with a superabundant response. In his earthly life—an earthly response to the heavenly Father—he showed us what it means to correspond to God. In other words, through the eternal life pulsating in him on earth he showed once and for all what the human response will be to the vision of God in eternity, what the integration of the human will with the divine will is to be like. No revelation of eternal life can be more important, more complete or more central than this one. Because the Son translated his life from eternity into time, we can conceive what it will be like when God translates our life from time into eternity.

When the first human beings began to mark the progress of time they had a benchmark in the divisions of day and night. In that context they could arrange their life and daily occurrences and express the duration of their feelings and experiences. They aged according to the measurement of time. There was a close connection between their life and transitory time. And they had to adapt themselves to time not only by counting the days but also by exploring the content of time, the seasons, months and years with their constant and changing elements, in order to adapt human activity to them. But besides these there were unchangeable attitudes, for the laws of God, including the natural laws governing man's own life, did not simply derive from time in spite of their link with perishableness. The goodness expressed in the law, for example the moral imperative, or the knowledge of God that was accessible to mankind were not as such fettered to time. Man was to fear God day or night, winter or summer. Certain things in existence were completely subject to time; nevertheless, there were relations with God and his eternity which admitted no fluctuation, though even this negative remained bound to the temporal form.

The appearance of the Son on earth burst asunder these rules, he who became man and yet was God. He had to adapt himself to the time which he had chosen for his earthly sojourn, yet at the same time he followed a law and a teaching that were heaven's own. He accepted the existing world without denying the existence of the superior world that was and remained more influential, and from which he was never separated, since he came in order to incarnate it on earth. He erected a vertical relationship between earth and heaven, which descended to earth in him. It was only the revelation of the Holy Spirit that spread heaven out horizontally in the world, once it had come to earth in the Son. Above all, the Son proclaimed the being of the heavenly Father, exalted above all, while the Spirit interpreted the Son by opening up the infinity of eternal life. The Son pointed to the height of heaven; the Spirit showed its breadth.

The first apostles knew the laws of the world and had the task of exploding each one, of expanding them and giving them new life through the Spirit. In their individual missions they were to proclaim the words of the Lord in such a way as to offer access even to unbelievers. Then Paul arrived on the scene and his duty was radically to burst the Law asunder, to show, in every earthly word and every accepted, limited concept, how eternal life exceeds all conceptualization. But no matter how much the Word showed itself to be the fullness of life in the preaching of Paul and all his followers up to the present day (so that every preacher can discover new aspects in it) their words always lead back, then as now, to the incarnate Son. His mere appearance was such a heavenly miracle, was such a conquest of the world by the Father, that it never ceases to be the living spring of truth, containing something absolute, unconditional and essential for every person living on earth. The consequences for man are that at this point (and at no other) the eternal life of the individual becomes concrete, palpable and accessible. Here the demands of God become explicit. And it is not a sublime game to distract him from his task as a human being; it is the whole gravity of the demands made by heaven on earth, looking for the Yes which each individual must speak to God in order to obtain what heaven has held in store for him from all eternity. Hence each person's mission is not something locked away in heaven for him, something of which he receives a weak foretaste on earth so that he may grope his way toward heaven (like a dog following a scent); rather it is sent down to him from heaven and it surrounds him like a voluminous garment. It comes clearly delineated from eternity and bestows on him his earthly task with a view to the same eternity. It derives and is dependent on the accomplished mission in heaven. Seen in this light grace is the accompaniment granted by the triune God from heaven to man, a gift which, in its perfect fullness, is located in God's eternal life, and which he constantly and prodigally pours out on earth; it is intended to help the faithful recognize here on earth the task given by heaven, cooperate in it and bring it back gratefully and confidently to God the Father, Son and Spirit as something which from all time has been given and recognized and has proceeded toward its fulfillment.

We know of two bodily ascensions into heaven: the Son's and the Mother's. We know that in the case of the Son he returns to his homeland, familiar to him from all eternity. He goes to the Father, where the Spirit continually mediates the exchange of love. As Love he returns to Love. In this return to the Father he leaves behind all the confinement and barriers imposed on him by his earthly life. But the essential determinant of his decision to become man stays with him: the love for mankind created by the Father, for each individual. This love is shown when the Son lets men share in the perfection of what he experienced on earth as well as in everything which he takes back to the Father at the end of his earthly sojourn. The Ascension is not the conclusion of his work of redemption; still less is it a turning away from the world now that it is redeemed. It is his humanity that he brings back to the Father in his Ascension, the same as our humanity, the common, catholic state of being human. This he brings home to heaven and finds everything as it was in eternity. His humanity does not feel a stranger in this home. In like manner our humanity is at home in heaven in the Son.

His Mother is taken up into heaven precisely as the person who she is: the person who said Yes in her love for the Son, the Father and the Spirit, she who lived out of the fullness of love and grace. As her Yes was completely fulfilled on earth through the coming of the Son, so this fullness is taken up into the plenitude reserved for her in heaven. Fullness is taken up into fullness; love which always exceeded all human love finds its final measure in the love of the glorified Son. This love is open infinity into which it grows without end. However, she who experiences this is still our Mother and one of us, embracing all her children in love. So far from leaving us behind and forgetting us, she finds us again in contemplating her Son.

We are sinners. We need to undergo in death a purification, a painful transformation. But we are accompanied both by the Son, who has found a place for us in his mission, and by the Mother, who goes to the Father with the Yes that she spoke for the entire human race. Hence every contemplation of the Lord and of his Mother is an invitation into eternal life. It is not an alien heaven, but rather the dwelling place of God, our homeland in faith. Every Yes uttered by man to the Son is laid up there. The Mother's Yes paved a broad road to heaven, so broad that no believer can miss it, but can follow the trail to the Son, to where he can exchange his perishable time for the eternal time of the triune God.

If man is ever able, in faith, to forget his human condition, his sins, his cares about existence, it happens when he is at prayer. While he prays he converses with the triune God in eternal life. Prayer possesses a breadth beyond the awareness of the one praying. This much he knows, that he is sharing in something mysterious and that his faith urges him to it and shows him the way—a way of his spirit's obedience to the Holy Spirit, of self-forgetfulness, of a nakedness which is equivalent to perfect poverty before God. He may form his prayer as he wills; but if it is profound enough, if it is placed entirely in the hands of the Father, then it is no longer his voice but the voice of the Church, a voice of mediation between heaven and earth. He probably experiences it best in the vista opened up by liturgical prayer, the supernatural conversation of the Church with God, of the priest with the Lord. It is a conversation of one who surrenders to the One who receives him. The Church understands the needs of man in her prayer; but she also recognizes the glory of God. She has charge of adoration, something which belongs to the whole Church in her unity. This adoration unites the prayers of the Old Covenant with the words of the Son and also with those of the saints and of the entire Church. Such a unity towers above the individual person at prayer and could never be reached by him, even in the most intense and ardent prayer; its ultimate purpose is to draw man along the path to eternal life. And the person who is thus drawn brings others with him, since liturgical prayer—and in the last analysis every prayer said selflessly and adoringly—is a word spoken from earth to heaven, the seeker's entrance into the now found kingdom of the Father. Two things come together in the Church's liturgy: the prayer which the Son spoke among us and taught to us, and the convergence of all praying hearts upon that one Word which he is and which encompasses the earth's hope: eternal life.